The Interview Question & Answer Book

The Interview Question & Answer Book

How to be ready to answer the
155 toughest interview questions

Second edition

James Innes

HIGH LIFE HIGHLAND	
3800 15 0043328 3	
Askews & Holts	Jan-2016
650.144	£10.99

PEARSON

Harlow, England • London • New York • Boston • San Francisco • Toronto • Sydney • Auckland • Singapore • Hong Kong
Tokyo • Seoul • Taipei • New Delhi • Cape Town • São Paulo • Mexico City • Madrid • Amsterdam • Munich • Paris • Milan

PEARSON EDUCATION LIMITED

Edinburgh Gate
Harlow CM20 2JE
United Kingdom
Tel: +44 (0)1279 623623
Web: www.pearson.com/uk

First published in Great Britain in 2012 (print), 2013 (electronic)
Second edition published 2016 (print and electronic)

© James Innes 2012 (print), 2013 (electronic)
© James Innes 2016 (print and electronic)

ISBN: 978-1-292-08655-2 (print)
       978-1-292-08657-6 (PDF)
       978-1-292-08656-9 (eText)
       978-1-292-08658-3 (ePub)

British Library Cataloguing-in-Publication Data
A catalogue record for this book is available from the British Library

Library of Congress Cataloging-in-Publication Data
Names: Innes, James, 1975- author.
Title: The interview question & answer book : how to be ready to answer the 155 toughest
    interview questions / James Innes.
Other titles: Interview question and answer book
Description: Second edition. | Harlow : Pearson Education, 2016. | Includes index.
Identifiers: LCCN 2015035189 | ISBN 9781292086552
Subjects: LCSH: Employment interviewing.
Classification: LCC HF5549.5.I6 I553 2016 | DDC 650.14/4—dc23
LC record available at http://lccn.loc.gov/2015035189

10 9 8 7 6 5 4 3 2 1
19 18 17 16

Cover design by redeyoffdesign.com, cover image © Treter/Shutterstock

Typeset in 10/13pt Mundo Sans Pro by Lumina Datamatics
Print edition printed in Malaysia (CTP-PJB)

NOTE THAT ANY PAGE CROSS REFERENCES REFER TO THE PRINT EDITION

Dedication

This book is dedicated to the small number of schoolmasters who, against all odds, actually managed to teach me something. I could say, 'They know who they are,' but they don't. (I was never very good at showing my gratitude to my teachers.) So I'd like to list them here, in alphabetical order: Tim Brandon-White (Latin; housemaster), Tom Brown (English), Michael Goldsworthy (History), Malcolm Innes (English; headmaster), David Oldman (History and Politics) and Nicholas Sudbury (Latin and Greek). Albert Einstein said, 'I never teach my pupils; I only attempt to provide the conditions in which they can learn.' All of these fine schoolmasters managed to do just that for me. I thank you all. (And a special plea to anyone who thinks they might know David Oldman: I have totally failed in my efforts to track him down and would appreciate any assistance! He taught me at Charterhouse around 1990. Please email me if you have any ideas: james.innes@jamesinnes.com)

Half of the author's royalties for this book will go to the Charlie Waller Memorial Trust (registered charity number 1109984), a charity which aims to raise awareness of the nature and dangers of depression. **Suicide is one of the three leading causes of death for teenagers and young adults under 25, an age group which accounts for almost a quarter of all suicides.** I encourage my readers to join me in supporting this important cause. Donations can be made online at **www.justgiving.com/charliewaller**.

Contents

About the author

James Innes is the founder and chairman of The CV Centre®, the UK's leading CV consultancy (**www.CVCentre.co.uk**) and part of the James Innes Group.

Following nearly two decades of experience heading up The CV Centre®, James is widely considered to be one of the UK's leading careers experts.

James regularly participates at recruitment fairs and conferences as a sought-after guest speaker, as well as being interviewed on TV and radio.

He is the author of a number of best-selling careers books. His current works are: *The CV Book, The Cover Letter Book, The Interview Book, The Interview Question & Answer Book* and *Ultimate New Job*.

Acknowledgements

I would like to thank all of my colleagues and clients at The CV Centre®, both present and past. Without them it would not have been possible for me to write *The Interview Question & Answer Book*. In particular, I would like to thank my Chief Executive Officer, Andy Dalziel, and our former Director of UK Operations, Susan Staley.

I would additionally like to thank Richard Day, our former Director of Technology, and Peter Anders Hvass, our Chief Technology Officer, for their significant contributions to the online elements of this book, and also Kirk Hullis, our Chief Marketing Officer, for his work on the promotion of the book.

Special thanks also go to the team at Pearson, in particular Eloise Cook, Emma Devlin, Paul East, Lesley Pummell, Dhanya Ramesh and the editorial services team at Lumina Datamatics, Lisa Robinson and Emma Steel. I couldn't have had better publishers behind me.

Assistance in checking and correcting the text was also provided by Michael Staley.

Thanks also to Steven Morrow for his suggestion of the interview question, "Is a tomato a vegetable?", Dan O'Brien for suggesting the last three questions in the book (and helping me with the answers!), Caroline Bristow for helping me to decide whether I'd rather fight a horse-sized duck or 100 duck-sized horses, Maria Rivington and Julie Sanders for helping me extensively with the remainder of the chapter on weird and wonderful questions and thanks also to Google, Microsoft, Capital Asset Exchange & Trading, UBS, Macquarie Bank and BHP Billiton for supplying me with some of those weird and wonderful questions!

Finally, I would like to thank my wife, Delphine Innes, and my daughter, Aleyna Innes, for their love and support and their toleration of my frequently working excessively long hours! Je vous aime . . .

Introduction

Dear Reader,

Why do some people almost always get the job they want?
Because they know precisely how to truly excel at interview!
Once your CV has been prepared and you have sent off your applications, the next stage on which to focus in securing the job you want is the interview phase.

Day in day out, I successfully coach my clients to truly excel at interview. This enables me to bring you the very best of what I have learned, helping you to excel at interview yourself.

So you've been invited for interview?

Your CV has been successful and you have been invited for interview; what next? People often think: 'Well, I'll just turn up and be myself,' which is fine, but it won't get you the job. You still have competition from the other applicants, so it's vital to plan and prepare for an interview; it's your key opportunity to make an impact. Your CV has helped get your foot in the door; you need to do the rest.

Why is it so important to plan and prepare?

The best person for the job, in terms of skills, experience and achievements, doesn't always pass the interview. The best person for the job doesn't always get the job. Sometimes the most able candidates on paper can really shoot themselves in the foot when they get to the interview.

The interview is one of the most critical points in the job search process. You might look great on paper, but you need to prove it to a recruiter. Many other factors that are not directly related to the person's ability to do the job are going to be picked up in the interview.

You've got the skills; now you need to demonstrate clearly that you'll be a good fit with your future co-workers and employers, and it's so easy to sabotage this valuable opportunity if you're unprepared.

On average, there are likely to be at least five other candidates being interviewed for the same vacancy. So, everything else being equal, you have a 20 per cent chance of getting the job. But there's so much you can do to improve your odds of success, and in *The Interview Question & Answer Book*, I'll help to give you that winning edge.

What can this book do to help you?

In *The Interview Question & Answer Book* I will show you how to develop a winning strategy. I will show you how to plan and prepare for a multitude of different interview questions, how to avoid cliché and how to really make an impact when handling both the classic questions and the really tough ones that interviewers can throw at you.

Once you are familiar with an interview question you can never again be stumped or surprised by it; being surprised in an interview is the last thing you want to happen. Surprise leads to pressure, pressure leads to stress, stress leads to panic, and panic can ruin your interview very quickly.

You'll find this book useful whether you are trying to land your first job, returning to the workplace after a career break or simply looking to take another step up the career ladder. *The Interview Question & Answer Book* condenses the same proven methodology I use every day with my clients and contains everything you need to handle all the questions you are likely to encounter.

Thank you for choosing *The Interview Question & Answer Book*. I have set out to write the most complete, definitive and up-to-date guide to interview questions (and how to answer them) on the market today. I trust you will both enjoy it and find it useful. And I look forward to meeting you in cyberspace should you have any further questions. Or maybe I'll have the opportunity to coach you one-on-one myself.

I really want to help you get the job and the future that you want.

Kind regards,

James Innes

James Innes
Twitter: @jamesinnes

Chairman, The CV Centre®
Author:
The CV Book
The Cover Letter Book
The Interview Book
The Interview Question & Answer Book
Ultimate New Job

Chapter **1**

Essential principles

Obviously, no one can know exactly what questions they will be asked at interview but there are certain topics that will almost certainly come up.

However, before we start looking at some of the possible questions you might be asked, I'd like to cover some important ground rules.

Listen

It's surprisingly easy for your thoughts to stray and for you to fail to properly listen to a question. You're in a stressful situation and you have a lot on your mind; it's perfectly possible to get distracted. If you do fail to hear a question, don't be afraid to ask the interviewer to repeat it. It's not ideal, but it's certainly better than failing to fully answer it, or guessing at what they've asked, going off at a tangent and giving the answer to a totally different question.

It's also possible that you fail to understand a question the first time round. Again, don't be afraid to ask the interviewer to repeat or to clarify their question. At the very least it gives you valuable extra thinking time. But don't make a habit of it!

Try to understand the meaning behind the question

Why have they asked you this question? What is it they are trying to find out?

I wouldn't go so far as to say that all interview questions have hidden meanings, but it is true that the intentions of the interviewer might not be immediately apparent from the question. If you can work out the meaning behind the question then you are at least 80 per cent of the way towards determining the optimum answer.

There are three key areas that an interviewer will be considering in their attempts to match a vacancy with the best possible candidate:

➤ Can you do the job? Do you have what it takes?

➤ Will you do the job? (Or will you just go through the motions?)

➤ Do you fit in with the other employees and the organisation as a whole?

All of their questions will address one of these three areas in one way or another. Therefore, in trying to understand the meaning behind any particular question you need to first identify which of the above areas the interviewer is trying to tackle.

Beyond that, you need to make sure you see the world from the interviewer's point of view. When asking you a particular question, what exactly is going through their mind?

Different types of question

As well as questions probing different areas, there are also different ways in which an interviewer might phrase their questions. You need to be aware of the different techniques they will use because these will impact on the way you answer.

In general terms, most questions can be classified as either 'open' or 'closed'.

A closed question is one which can be answered very quickly, often with just one word:

➤ Are you creative?

➤ Do you thrive under pressure?

➤ Are you a risk taker?

➤ Do you have sales experience?

An open question is one which will force a lengthier answer:

➤ In what ways would you say that you are creative?

➤ Can you tell me about a time when you were under significant pressure and how you handled that?

➤ How do you feel about taking risks?

➤ Can you tell me about your sales experience?

A good interviewer will normally ask mainly open questions because these are the questions which will extract the most useful information from you. Conversely, a poor interviewer is likely to ask you a much higher proportion of closed questions.

Regardless of the type of question (or interviewer) you're faced with, you should always avoid 'Yes' and 'No' answers to questions unless you're sure it's appropriate as they tend to be conversation stoppers.

Leading questions

Another type of question you are likely to encounter is a 'leading' question:

➤ What character flaws do you have?

➤ Why haven't you achieved more in your career?

➤ You must surely have more than one weakness?

You can see that these questions, whilst open, nevertheless lead you down a very specific path. The interviewer isn't asking you whether or not you have any character flaws; in delivering a leading question they're making it clear they have inherently assumed that you do indeed have character flaws. Leading questions are definitely something you need to keep a close lookout for.

You should also note that a leading question doesn't always have to be an open question. By posing you a leading question, which is also a closed question, an interviewer can really put you on the spot:

➤ I think you're overqualified for this job. Don't you?

But don't worry because I'll show you how to deal with this in Chapter 4: The top 25 tough questions: taking the heat.

Funnel interviewing

A final interviewing technique I'd like to make you aware of is so-called 'funnel' interviewing.

In funnel interviewing, an interviewer will first pose you a very general question about a topic (potentially lulling you into a false sense of security) before following up their original question with more and more precise questions (often based on your previous answers) on the same topic until they've got you talking about precisely what interests them.

Although it's a technique popular with interrogators, it's not normally as frightening as it sounds. It all depends on the interviewer. Generally their supplementary questions will follow a fairly mundane sequence, starting with the favourite, 'Can you give me an example?'

The secret to handling this technique is to be aware of it and to make sure you don't let the interviewer force you into revealing anything that's not to your advantage. Just remember one of the essentials of good interview technique: EBBOM – engage brain before opening mouth!

Pause to give yourself the necessary time to construct an answer so that you answer the question to the best of your ability. If you've prepared properly – and both this and the following chapters should help you to do just that – then it's unlikely their question will come as too much of a shock to you. You should already have an answer more or less ready.

However, if you're taken aback by their question, give yourself a few seconds before starting to respond. That should be just long enough to get your head round the question and will make a big difference to the quality of your answer.

Keep your answer on track

Make sure that you answer questions fully without waffling or chattering on unnecessarily. Nervousness can cause you to say too much and to give too much away.

The power of silence

Silence has been used to great effect by leaders, journalists, negotiators and interviewers, as a technique for getting people to reveal more than they should. Watch out for it being used. It will happen like this: you provide an answer to their question, but instead of immediately following up with another question they will just sit there silently. Human nature, added to your already nervous state, will make you carry on talking, either elaborating on or rephrasing your existing answer to fill the awkward silence.

Psychotherapists also use silence as a key tool. They are trained to say very little, which forces their client to open up and disclose more.

Whilst this might be very useful for someone undergoing psychotherapy, it's likely to cause you to come unstuck in an interview.

Now you are aware of this technique, don't fall into the trap.

An interviewer is especially likely to adopt this tactic after a question such as, 'What are your weaknesses?' The more they can keep you talking, the more you're likely to reveal.

Back up your answers with real-life examples

Wherever possible you should try to integrate real-life examples into your answers, rather than just speaking hypothetically. Flagging up specific relevant examples from your own experience is an ideal way of reinforcing your points in the interviewer's mind.

TOP TIP

If the interviewer asks you a straightforward question without specifically requesting you to give an example, then don't hesitate to be proactive and give them an example anyway.

I've already made the point that many interviewers will start with a simple question and then probe the topic further by following up with another question such as, 'Can you give me an example?'

If you pre-empt this by illustrating your initial response with an example then it's bound to impress them.

Delivering sound bites

If you ever watch a politician or a senior businessperson being interviewed on television, you will notice that they all have a little trick up their sleeves. If they've received any kind of debate or media training, they will be adept at making sure they get their point across regardless of the question being asked.

This is especially so when they're discussing particularly sensitive topics or when confronted with a particularly aggressive interviewer. In his famous interview with politician Michael Howard, interviewer Jeremy

Paxman asked exactly the same question ('Did you threaten to overrule him?') a total of 12 times without getting a straight answer!

You should not be this evasive; it didn't do much for Michael Howard's reputation and it won't do much for yours. However, if you are able to subtly steer a question round to dodge an issue you are uncomfortable about, and deliver a pre-prepared statement you have been keen to make, then it can be a very effective technique. But use it sparingly.

You may not be answering the precise question you have been asked but you should be addressing the topic that the interviewer has raised. You're simply doing so in the manner which suits you best.

The truth, the whole truth . . .

Never lie at interview or say something that you cannot substantiate.

For many candidates their troubles start even before they've been invited for the interview because a large percentage of people seem to think it's permissible to tell a few small porkies when writing their CV because everyone else does it and many prospective employers do not check an applicant's information as thoroughly as they perhaps should.

However, I would always strongly caution anyone against telling anything but the truth on their CV. You can easily become unstuck during an interview as a result.

BLOOPER!

One candidate claimed to be fluent in French on his CV and then got quite a shock when he came up against a half-French/half-English interviewer who thought it quite reasonable to conduct the interview in French.

And this is a surprisingly common cause of pre-interview jitters: worrying about whether or not you are going to be unmasked as a liar.

STATISTIC

Surveys show that approximately 30 per cent of candidates 'lie' to one degree or another at interview.

Of course, it all depends on how you define 'lie'. Twenty per cent engage in a 'significant' lie (the kind where you could later be sacked for gross misconduct as a result), whereas up to 35 per cent include at least one small porky here or there.

But just because 'everyone else does it' doesn't mean that you should. Not everyone lies – it remains a minority – and it is very questionable whether those that do gain any benefit from it.

Whether or not you tell the whole truth, though, is another matter entirely. Clearly you should always put as positive a spin as possible on matters but it's a fine line, and only you can be the judge of what is and is not acceptable.

Don't be a parrot

An essential warning to all readers:

I will be giving you example answers to a whole variety of questions, but I must emphasise that it is vitally important for you to think through and write out your own answers. Once I have fully explained the meaning behind the question and given you my pointers on how to develop your answer, then it shouldn't be too difficult for you to do so.

My examples are there purely to help illustrate the points made, to act as a guide only; most are unlikely to fit your precise circumstances exactly. It's essential for you to think for yourself and to create your own answers; my job is purely to help you achieve that.

This will take time and effort on your part but it is absolutely vital as your answers must come across as genuine. It's time and effort that will really pay dividends. You'll feel so much more confident.

Too many candidates at interview make the mistake of sounding as if they're reciting from some old-fashioned book called *101 Interview Questions*.

Make sure you don't fall into this trap. This is really important. There are no universally right answers to interview questions, just answers that are right for *you*; I will help you to work out what those right answers should be.

Even if you have prepared and memorised your answers, you should be careful to make sure that your delivery is natural, not stilted, and doesn't come across as rehearsed. This is especially important with the more difficult and challenging questions. If you don't express any surprise and answer perfectly and without hesitation, then it's going to look rather suspicious.

Preparing and practising your answers

To help you in preparing and practising your answers to the questions covered in this book, we have developed an online tool which will present you with random questions and give you the opportunity to write your answers and save them for later use as a revision tool. To access this really useful tool, please visit the following website:

www.jamesinn.es

Taking the time to think through and create your answers is definitely the very best way to prepare.

Chapter **2**

The top 10 interview questions

Here's my list of what I consider to be the top 10 questions you are likely to be asked at interview. You should think very carefully about your answers to all these questions before getting anywhere near an interview room.

1 Can you tell me a bit about yourself?

2 Why have you applied for this vacancy?

3 Why do you wish to leave your current position?

4 Why do you want to work for this organisation?

5 What are your strengths?

6 What are your weaknesses?

7 What has been your greatest achievement/accomplishment?

8 What can you, above all the other applicants, bring to this job?

9 Where do you see yourself in five years' time?

10 You've mentioned x under the Interests & Activities on your CV. Can you tell me a bit more about that?

You are absolutely certain to get asked at least some of these questions (or variations of them), if not the whole lot.

We'll look at them one by one, alongside possible alternatives and other closely related questions. We'll analyse the interviewer's intentions in asking you the question – the meaning behind the question – and we'll discuss how best you can answer it.

1. Can you tell me a bit about yourself?

Alternative and related questions

Can you talk me through your CV?

The meaning behind the question

This is an extremely popular question, and is just the kind an interviewer might throw at you at the beginning of an interview to get the ball rolling. They are placing you centre stage and hoping you will open up to them. Alternatively, they're hopelessly overworked, haven't yet had time to read your CV, and asking you this question will buy them some breathing space!

Your answer

This is a very broad question and you might be at a loss as to the approach you should take to answering it.

They're not asking for an autobiography. Focus on discussing major selling points that feature on your CV or application form, selling points which are directly relevant to the job for which you are applying. Don't start telling them your whole life history.

Whilst they do want you to open up to them and paint a picture of you, you're not on the psychiatrist's couch; keep it professional and avoid getting too personal.

Besides talking about your career, make sure you have something to say about your education and qualifications, and even your hobbies and interests.

It's vital to practise your answer for this in advance, and to try to limit your answer to one minute. If you can't successfully 'pitch' yourself in under a minute then you're going to risk losing the interviewer's attention.

How have you described yourself in the *Professional profile* at the top of your CV? A lot of this material can be recycled to help you draft your answer to this question.

EXAMPLE

I'm a highly driven individual with extensive management experience acquired principally in the aviation sector. Following completion of my degree in international business, which included a couple of years in Germany, I started my career in administration and have worked my way up to become an export sales manager. I believe I combine a high level of commercial awareness with a commitment to customer care, which helps me to achieve profitable growth in a competitive market. I enjoy being part of as well as managing, motivating, training and developing a successful and productive team and I thrive in highly pressurised and challenging working environments. I have strong IT skills, I'm fluent in German and I'm also a qualified first aider. In my spare time I undertake a wide range of activities; I'm particularly keen on squash and I am also currently working towards my Private Pilot Licence.

2. Why have you applied for this vacancy?

Alternative and related questions

Why do you want this vacancy?
What attracted you to this vacancy?
Why do you think you're suitable for this job?
What is it that you are looking for in a new job?

The meaning behind the question

The interviewer is probing to see:

➤ if you fully understand what the job entails;

➤ how well you might match their requirements;

➤ what appeals to you most about the job.

Your answer

This is another open-ended question where you might be tempted to say too much. By taking the time to think through your answer in advance, you will be able to remain focused on a few key points.

Your emphasis should be on demonstrating to the interviewer precisely how you match their requirements, and that you fully understand what the role entails.

If you've done your research properly then you will have a good idea of what it is they are looking for.

They have asked you what your motivations are in applying for the vacancy, but try to turn the question round so that the answer you give tells them why you are the right candidate for the vacancy.

EXAMPLE

I've applied for this vacancy because it's an excellent match for my skills and experience and because it represents a challenge, which I know I'll relish. I already have extensive experience as a senior quantity surveyor, including previous experience of rail and station projects, an area I'm particularly interested in. I enjoy managing multiple projects simultaneously. I also enjoy overseeing and coaching junior and assistant quantity surveyors. I'm used to dealing directly with clients; developing productive working relationships with clients is definitely one of my strengths. This role is exactly the sort of role I am currently targeting and I am confident I will be able to make a major contribution.

3. Why do you wish to leave your current position?

Alternative and related questions

Why do you wish to leave your current employer?
What do you plan to say to your current employer in your letter of resignation?

The meaning behind the question

The interviewer is trying to understand your motivation to change jobs; they also want to know how serious you are about changing jobs. Are you really committed to moving or are you just wasting their time?

Your answer

There are a multitude of reasons for wanting to leave your job, but they won't all be positive selling points for you.
Positive reasons include:

➤ Wanting a greater challenge.

➤ Wanting to diversify.

➤ Seeking greater opportunities.

➤ Seeking further advancement.

➤ Taking a step up the career ladder.

Negative reasons include:

➤ Problems with your boss.

➤ Problems with a colleague.

➤ A financially unstable organisation.

➤ Personal reasons.

If your reason for wanting to leave your job is a positive one then your answer will be easy enough to construct. Explain to the interviewer what your motivations are and how the move to your next job will help you to achieve your goals. You are making a positive move for positive reasons and intend to achieve a positive outcome, simple as that.

If, however, your reason for leaving your job is in my list of negative reasons, then giving the right answer is going to be somewhat trickier. Because each of the situations is so different, I will deal with each of them in turn.

Problems with your boss: Having problems with the boss is the top reason people give (in surveys) for changing jobs. However, you should never say anything negative about either a current or a previous employer. It isn't professional; it doesn't portray you as someone who is particularly loyal and it will reflect badly on you.

I would recommend that you avoid citing this as a reason. Criticising your current employer is considered one of the top mistakes you can make at interview and will most likely cost you the job regardless of whether or not your criticism is justified. Aim to give an answer which focuses on the benefits you will experience in moving to your new job rather than making any reference to your having had problems with your boss.

BLOOPER!

Having delivered a particularly devastating critique of their current employer, one candidate was shocked to discover that their current employer was in fact the interviewer's brother-in-law.

Problems with a colleague: Maybe you want to leave because of a persistently unpleasant colleague. However, explaining this to the interviewer will most likely open you up to expressing bitterness or recrimination, traits that are not attractive to a potential employer. Again, you should aim to give an answer which focuses on the benefits of moving to your new job, rather than drawing attention to your problems.

A financially unstable organisation: You may well have decided to leave your job before your employer goes bankrupt, but you don't want to be labelled as a rat leaving a sinking ship. It doesn't say much for your loyalty. Avoid giving this as a reason.

Personal reasons: There are many personal circumstances which might cause you to wish to leave a job. For example, you might want a better work–life balance. However, if possible you should avoid giving personal reasons as an answer and instead leave the interviewer to believe you are leaving in order to pursue a more promising opportunity.

As for asking what you would write in a resignation letter, you should remember that when it comes to resignation letters, it is well worth being as nice as possible about the matter. Harsh words in a letter of resignation could easily come back to haunt you in the future, not least if you ever need a reference out of that employer.

EXAMPLE

I would simply tell them that, after careful consideration, I have made the decision to move on to a new challenge. Naturally, I'd thank them for the opportunities with which they presented me during the course of my employment, reassure them that I will, of course, do my best to help ensure the seamless transfer of my duties and responsibilities before leaving, and wish them all the very best for the future.

---

4. Why do you want to work for this organisation?

Alternative and related questions

What is it about our organisation that attracts you?

The meaning behind the question

The interviewer is analysing your motivations and probing your expectations of their organisation. Why do you want to work for them in particular? Whilst this question doesn't directly ask what you know about their organisation, in order to be able to answer it effectively you are going to have to demonstrate that you have done your homework.

Your answer

BLOOPER!

One interviewee answered this question by saying, 'Because you're in Mayfair.' He didn't get the job.

If you have done your research you will be fairly well informed as to the organisation you are applying to join. However, the key to answering this question is how to communicate that knowledge to the interviewer whilst tying it in with why you want to work for them.

Your focus should be on what in particular attracts you to their organisation. We'll cover the closely related but more generalised question, 'What do you know about us as an organisation?' in the next chapter.

> **EXAMPLE**
>
> I'm particularly attracted by how progressive an organisation you are. I've seen how your sales levels have grown the past few years and I'm aware of your plans to expand into the United States. Yours is an organisation which is rapidly developing and evolving and that's exactly what I'm looking for. I want to work for an organisation which is forward-thinking and isn't afraid to tackle new challenges.

5. What are your strengths?

Alternative and related questions

What are you good at?
What do you consider yourself to be good at?

The meaning behind the question

With this question the interviewer wants to achieve the following:

➤ Identify what your key selling points are.

➤ Establish whether or not these strengths are relevant to the role they are interviewing for.

➤ Gain some insight into your character – how self-confident (or arrogant) you are.

Your answer

Everyone has strengths. The key to answering this question is not to rattle off a long list of what you consider your strengths to be. Instead you should highlight a smaller number of specific strengths, which will be most appealing to the company. Discuss each one briefly, and, most importantly, identify how these strengths relate to the requirements of the job you are applying to undertake. You can even elaborate on one of your strengths by mentioning a specific relevant achievement.

Choose your strengths carefully. It can be hard to say anything very interesting, for example, about the fact that you are very meticulous and pay great attention to detail. However, if the recruiter is looking for someone to lead a team then you can mention team leadership as one of your strengths and cite an appropriate example or achievement.

EXAMPLE

I believe my key strength is that I combine experience of traditional film production with extensive experience in the online arena. I'm very aware of current trends in new media and am able to demonstrate excellent creative judgement. I'm also very good at juggling multiple projects simultaneously; in my current role I frequently have as many as half a dozen different projects on the go at any one time, and I'm committed to completing them all on time and on budget. This clearly requires extremely strong project management skills.

Word of warning
If you don't give the interviewer at least one example to back up your statement, then be prepared for them to ask you for one.

6. What are your weaknesses?

Alternative and related questions

What are you not good at doing?
What do you find difficult to do and why?
In what areas do you feel you need to improve?

The meaning behind the question

With questions of this kind the interviewer wants to achieve the following:

➤ Identify any weakness which might be detrimental to your ability to undertake the role.

> See how you react when faced with a somewhat tricky question.

> Assess how self-aware you are and how you define weakness.

Your answer

Some might consider this a tough interview question and think it should be in Chapter 4. But believe me, there are much tougher questions than this! I would only classify this question as tricky rather than tough. Whilst it is superficially a somewhat negative question it is in fact full of opportunities for you to turn it round to your advantage and make your answer a positive point.

Don't be perturbed by the question or let it throw you off balance. Your answer should be right on the tip of your tongue because we will work on it right now. The first thing to make clear is that you should only ever discuss a professional weakness, unless the interviewer specifically requests otherwise (unlikely).

Your first thought might be that you are tempted to say, 'I don't really have any particular weaknesses.' But this is definitely not the answer the interviewer is looking for and is definitely not the answer you should be giving them.

BLOOPER!

Telling the interviewer your weakness is 'Kryptonite', as one candidate did, is unlikely to amuse an interviewer.

The interviewer wants to know that you are able to look at yourself objectively and criticise yourself where appropriate. If you honestly don't think you have any weaknesses then you risk coming across as arrogant if you say so, and no one wants a perfect candidate anyway.

You don't want to come up with a straightforward list of what you consider your weaknesses to be, so you have two choices:

> Talk about a weakness that's not necessarily a weakness at all.

> Talk about a weakness that you turned (or can turn) into a strength.

The problem with the first option is that you risk running into serious cliché territory:

I would have to say that my main weakness is that I'm a perfectionist.

I have a reputation for working too hard; I often push myself far too hard in my work.

You risk sounding like you plucked your answer straight out of a 1990s manual on interview technique.

Personally, I prefer the second option: Talk about a weakness that you turned (or are turning) into a strength.

You are answering the interviewer's question by highlighting a definite weakness, but you then go on to reflect positively on this by outlining the active steps you have taken or are taking to overcome it. You are demonstrating a willingness to learn, adapt and improve and you are demonstrating that you have the initiative required to make changes where changes are due.

Choosing a weakness that has its root in lack of experience and has been (or is being) overcome by further training is ideal because it is a weakness that is relatively easily resolved.

EXAMPLE

When I first started my current job my first few months were an uphill battle dealing with a backlog of work I inherited from my predecessor. I recognised that I have a weakness when it comes to time management. I have since been on a time management course, read a couple of books on the subject and I believe I've made a lot of progress. But it's something I'm still very vigilant of. I make a concerted effort to apply the principles I've learned every day, and to put in place procedures which enable me to most effectively prioritise and process my workload.

This is a good and comprehensive answer meeting all of the objectives we've outlined above.

Word of warning
Be prepared for the interviewer to ask the follow-up question, 'OK. That's one weakness. You must surely have more than one weakness?' We'll cover this question in Chapter 4: The top 25 tough questions: taking the heat.

7. What has been your greatest achievement/accomplishment?

Alternative and related questions

What are your biggest achievements?
What are you most proud of?
What was your biggest achievement in your current/last job?
What has been the high point of your career so far?

The meaning behind the question

Unless they qualify the question by specifically mentioning, for example, your last job, it is important to remember that the interviewer isn't necessarily looking for a work-related achievement. They are looking for evidence of achievement, full stop. However, a work-related achievement is normally what they'll be expecting.

Your answer

You'll want to make sure you have thought through this question carefully before the interview and have selected both a key professional achievement as well as a key personal achievement; cover both bases.

Try not to go too far back; try to pick a recent achievement. If you've included an *Achievements* section in your CV (which I would recommend you do), then this will be a good starting point for you to generate ideas.

Describe clearly to the interviewer:

➤ what it is that you achieved;

➤ what the background and circumstances were;

➤ what impact it had on your career/life.

What was the benefit? Try to phrase this in such a way for it to be self-evident that this would also be a benefit to any prospective employer.

EXAMPLE

My greatest achievement so far would probably be winning the Manager of the Year award last year. I made numerous operational changes at my branch, including a massive reduction in stock levels, which significantly boosted our working capital. I also drove up sales levels, especially by increasing the uptake of after-sales insurance packages. The net effect was that we smashed the previous branch sales record by an impressive 37 per cent, and profits rose in line with this. This directly resulted in my promotion to the management of the flagship Edinburgh branch.

8. What can you, above all the other applicants, bring to this job?

Alternative and related questions

What makes you the best candidate for this job?

The meaning behind the question

The interviewer is directly asking you what your unique selling point is. They're looking for at least one significant reason that you should be their No. 1 choice for the job.

Your answer

Well, what does make you the best candidate for this job?

I'll level with you; this isn't necessarily a top 10 question in terms of how likely you are to get asked it. However, it is very much a top 10 question in terms of the importance of your having prepared an answer to it. You need to go into each and every interview with a thorough understanding of what it is that you have to offer. If you don't know what it is that you're offering then how can you hope to be able to sell it effectively?

If you do get asked this question then don't be afraid to answer it candidly. It's a bold question and warrants a bold answer. The interviewer is really putting you on the spot to sell yourself. But do be very careful to avoid coming across as arrogant because that's the last thing you want to do. It's a fine line you need to tread.

Feel free to cite an example from your past where you demonstrated that you are someone who is capable of going the extra mile. It's all very well to say that you're someone who gives 100 per cent (although it is a bit of a cliché), but if you can throw an example at your interviewer then you're going to be a whole lot more credible.

BLOOPER!

....

One ex-army candidate for a management role replied, 'I can shoot someone at 300 yards.' What is more amazing is that the person actually got the job! This is a rare example of a sense of humour working to the candidate's advantage.

EXAMPLE

Having now been working in this industry for over a decade, I have developed successful relationships with key decision makers in numerous companies, enabling me to achieve a sales conversion rate much higher than average. This is undoubtedly a very challenging role, requiring considerable drive and determination, but I believe my previous sales record is clear evidence that I am more than capable of achieving what it is that you need.

---

9. Where do you see yourself in five years' time?

Alternative and related questions

How long do you plan to stay/would you stay in this job if we offer it to you?
What are your long-term career goals?
How does this job fit into your long-term career plans?
How far do you feel you might rise in our organisation?

The meaning behind the question

The interviewer is trying to ascertain what your long-term career ambitions are. They want to get a better understanding of your motivations. They will normally be looking for someone who is keen to learn, develop and progress. However, they are recruiting for a specific role and they will want someone who is prepared to commit to that role for a reasonable period of time.

You may think this question is just a cliché and doesn't really get asked in practice. Trust me it does, far more frequently than you might imagine.

Your answer

Yes, lots of people will think they're displaying a great sense of humour/ ambition/self-confidence to reply, 'Doing your job!' I wouldn't recommend it, though because it will come across as arrogant and aggressive.

Avoid being too specific. It's very difficult for most people to know exactly what job they will be undertaking in five years' time and so it can come across as unrealistic to quote a specific job title you are aiming for. Try to present your answer more in terms of what level you hope you will have reached; what level of responsibility, of autonomy. It's also a good idea if you can phrase your answer to communicate that you hope you will still be with this same organisation in five years' time.

EXAMPLE

Five years from now I expect I will have progressed significantly in my career and be making an even greater contribution. Having proved my value to the organisation I would hope to have been given increased responsibilities and greater challenges. I've clearly given a good deal of thought to working for you and I can see that there are a lot of opportunities both for promotion and for ongoing professional development. My career is very important to me and I want to push myself hard to deliver the very best of which I'm capable.

10. You've mentioned x under the *Interests & Activities* on your CV. Can you tell me a bit more about that?

Alternative and related questions

What activities do you enjoy outside work?

What are you interested in outside work?

The meaning behind the question

There are a variety of possible reasons an interviewer might ask this question:

➤ They're trying to get some insight into your personality and character.

➤ They're testing to see how truthful you've been on your CV.

➤ They've run out of other questions and are killing time!

Besides knowing whether you're capable of actually doing the job, most employers are keen to know what sort of a person you would be like to work alongside. Employers are generally keen to have a diversity of characters within their team and are always on the lookout for someone who can add a new dimension.

Whilst nobody has yet conducted a survey specifically to research this, there is plenty of anecdotal evidence of recruiters deciding to call someone in for an interview purely as a result of what they've included on their CV under *Interests & Activities*. I, for one, will admit to having done so when hiring.

Your answer

This is a very simple question to answer, provided that you've prepared for it in advance. If you have a hobby that makes for an interesting talking point at the interview then it will reflect positively on you as an individual.

You should be able to back up anything you've listed on your CV. If you mention chess to give your CV some intellectual clout but haven't actually played since you were at school, then you could come a cropper in your interview if your interviewer turns out to be a chess fan and asks you which openings to the game you favour.

It's always a good idea if you can subtly slip in mention of any positions of responsibility you hold outside work. If your passion is, for example, football and you are also the captain of the local team, then say so.

Besides the obvious selling point of football being a team activity (and hence your being a team player), you've immediately communicated your leadership qualities, your ability to take responsibility for others, your ability to commit yourself to a project etc.

EXAMPLE

I've always been fascinated by planes. I remember my first flight as a child; it was a thrilling experience. Even though I understand the science behind it, I'm still in awe each and every time I see a plane clear the runway. It's quite an expensive hobby to pursue, but as soon as I could afford to do so, I started taking flying lessons. I gained my Private Pilot Licence, went on to qualify as an instructor and I'm now a senior member of my local flying club. Whilst it's not something I've ever wished to pursue as a career, I do enjoy giving the occasional lesson and generally participating in the club community. It's definitely something about which I'm very passionate.

Chapter **3**

Fifty more classic questions: be prepared

There are many interview question books, which feature hundreds of different questions and answers. Whilst you might have time to quickly read through them, you're unlikely to have the time or the inclination to look at any of them in any great depth, nor to think through your own answers.

If you look closely at all these questions you'll see that many of them are simply variations on a theme and that the same core themes come up again and again. There are so many different ways to word a question but only a limited number of topics the interviewer is likely to be interested in.

I believe that rather than spoon-feeding you the answers to questions it's much more important for you to recognise and fully understand the different lines of questioning an interviewer is likely to take.

Within each individual theme there will be a cluster of closely related questions all attempting to address the same issue.

I have condensed hundreds of interview questions down to a list of 50 questions, which cover pretty much every key issue an interviewer is likely to tackle you on. We'll be looking at these in detail in this chapter.

So-called 'tough' questions

Many questions which you might, at first sight, consider to be 'tough' are actually nothing more than alternatively and more aggressively phrased versions of classic questions.

For example, instead of asking you the relatively innocuous question, 'How far do you feel you might rise in our organisation?' your interviewer, if they're the sadistic sort, might ask you, 'Would you like to have my job?'

Clearly there will be differences in how you respond to each of these questions but the core answer is the same.

I'm not saying that tough questions don't exist; they most certainly do (and we'll be covering them in the next chapter). But most of the questions you're likely to encounter, which might traditionally be seen as tough, really aren't that tough at all once you've understood what it is the interviewer is driving at. If you can see through to the meaning behind the question then it can take a lot of the sting out of a question.

1. How would you describe yourself? How would your boss/colleagues/team/family/ friends describe you?

Alternative and related questions

What do you think your references will say about you?
What kind of person are you to work with?

The meaning behind the question

The interviewer wants to assess how you perceive yourself. Whether they ask how you would describe yourself or how others would describe you, their question is all about seeing yourself as others see you.

Your answer

This is a very popular question and could conceivably have made my top 10. It's vital to be prepared for it.

You will want to make sure you have a few well-chosen adjectives up your sleeve ready to answer this question, e.g. loyal, dedicated, ambitious, determined, independent, highly motivated, understanding etc. Tell the interviewer what they want to hear. But don't be too big-headed; a little modesty can go a long way.

It's a difficult balance to strike, but I hope the following example will show you how to achieve this.

EXAMPLE

I would describe myself as a very determined and highly moti-vated person. I do take my job seriously, but I'm able to see things in perspective and believe I'm quite easy-going to work with. I'm an optimist rather than a pessimist, but I'm also a realist and I cope well when the going gets tough; I'm very good at finding solutions to problems. Above all, I would say I'm a positive and enthusiastic person, and I relish a challenge.

Word of warning

There's no need to back up this answer with examples, such as outlining a time when you were particularly understanding with a colleague. It would be going too far.

---

2. In what ways are you a team player?

Alternative and related questions

Do you prefer working on your own or as part of a team?

How would you define teamwork?

Can you tell me about a team you worked in and the role you played within that team?

What do you think makes a perfect team?

The meaning behind the question

Teamwork is essential in almost every work environment; therefore, questioning your ability to work in a team is one of an interviewer's favourites. They'll be looking for evidence of a number of core abilities:

➤ The ability to communicate effectively with others.

➤ The ability to recognise and understand the viewpoints of others.

➤ The ability to appreciate the contribution you are expected to make.

Your answer

This is a very important and very popular question, which could be phrased in many different ways. As well as pre-preparing your answer to: 'In what ways are you a team player?' you should also draft answers to all the alternative questions I've listed above. There will be common ground between your answers but each will have a slightly different slant to it.

You could answer the question in the context of your current job but you'd be better off approaching it from the angle of the job for which you are applying. They're asking you in what ways you are a team player, but you need to be asking yourself in what ways will *they want* you to be a team player. Are they looking for a leader? Are they looking for someone who brings out the best in others? Are they looking for the person who generates the ideas or the person who is a dab hand at putting new ideas into practice?

Establish in your own mind what sort of a team player they want you to be and then deliver an answer which caters to that image.

EXAMPLE

I very much enjoy working with others; I'm outgoing, I enjoy the team spirit and I'm understanding of the needs of others. I'm good at helping the team to see the bigger picture; to see the wood from the trees, helping them to focus on what really matters rather than getting bogged down in irrelevant detail. I'm also good at helping the team to spot flaws in our approach and potential problems and pitfalls. I believe I have strong communication skills, and whilst I don't yet have experience in a leadership role, I do have a talent for liaising between different team members and resolving any disputes which may arise. Conflict between different team members is rarely very productive and is normally best avoided.

---

3. Do you work well on your own initiative?

Alternative and related questions

Are you able to manage your own workload?

The meaning behind the question

Given the choice between someone who can be left to get on with a job and someone who needs constant supervision, who would you hire?

Employees who work well on their own initiative are highly prized.

With this question, the interviewer is seeking evidence that you are such an employee.

Your answer

Of course you work well on your own initiative. But how can you prove that to the interviewer? This is a closed question but it certainly requires more than a one-word answer. It's a great chance for you to roll out a pre-prepared example, which ticks all the interviewer's boxes and shows you in a positive light.

If the interviewer is asking you this question, the chances are that will be expected to be able to work on your own initiative. If you've carefully studied the job description you should be able to identify under what circumstances this will be required. Choosing an example from a past (or present) job which closely matches these circumstances is going to have a much stronger impact.

EXAMPLE

I enjoy working with others but I'm equally able to work on my own initiative. I'm not afraid to ask for guidance if necessary but I'm quick to learn, and once I've understood what's required of me I am more than capable of getting on with the job under my own steam. In my current role I work as part of a close-knit team but that's not to say that there aren't certain tasks and projects I have to handle on my own. For example, I have sole responsibility for reconciling credits and debits on our bank statements to our sales and purchase ledgers. It's not a task that can be shared with anyone; it's not a two-man job. I set aside one day a week to concentrate on this because it does require a lot of concentration, reconciling entries which match and taking steps to resolve any discrepancies.

Word of warning

Even if you do prefer to work on your own, it's best not to mention this. You don't want to risk being labelled 'not a team player'. This question doesn't ask whether you prefer to work on your own; it simply asks how capable you are of doing so.

4. What techniques do you use to get things done?

Alternative and related questions

How do you get things done at work?

The meaning behind the question

This is a very simple question. The interviewer wants to know what your working style is; how do you plan and organise yourself to ensure that you achieve your objectives? They don't just want to hear you say that you're a very organised and efficient person; they want proof of exactly how you get things done.

Your answer

Tell it like it is. The interviewer isn't expecting any magic tricks or a treatise on the latest management techniques. Your answer just needs to outline the systems and tools you use to manage your workload to ensure that everything which needs to get done does get done. You should aim to emphasise that the techniques you use are ones which work for you.

EXAMPLE

Careful planning is critical to my ability to get things done: planning, organisation and action. I rely heavily on 'To Do' lists. These enable me to capture and record everything which I need to action. I maintain a master To Do list but also have separate To Do lists for each particular project I'm handling. I review these at least once a day to identify my priorities. I always aim to focus on tasks which have deadlines attached to them and also tasks which will achieve the most in the shortest space of time. Less important items I will either postpone, delegate, or, if I am unable to clearly identify the benefits, remove from the list completely. Whilst I have a very heavy workload to juggle I find that these systems enable me to always keep one step ahead and to ensure that nothing slips through the net.

---

5. What motivates you?

Alternative and related questions

What do you need to retain your motivation?

The meaning behind the question

What the interviewer is really asking is, 'What would we have to do to motivate you?' and 'Would you be sufficiently motivated to undertake this job effectively?' They're unlikely to ask this directly, though. By asking you the more open-ended, 'What motivates you?' they're likely to extract a lot more useful information out of you, if you are careless enough to let them have it. Interviewers want to hire highly motivated people, not people who are just going to go through the motions until it's time to go home.

Your answer

There are lots of different things which could motivate you. You've got to be careful to pick factors:

➤ which will reflect positively on you as an individual;

➤ which are not inconsistent with the job for which you are applying;

➤ which are equally of benefit to your prospective employer;

➤ which will not impose any kind of a burden on the employer.

I'm not going to hide the fact that money is a major motivator. It's the primary reason most people go to work each day. However, unless you are in sales or some other highly money-driven and largely commission-based role, then you should steer clear of mentioning money as a motivating factor. It's too selfish an answer. It's a factor which is purely in your own interests and not your prospective employer's.

I would recommend that, depending on the nature of the role, you cite factors such as challenges, results and recognition and elaborate on these to demonstrate their value to the employer.

EXAMPLE

I'm very results-driven. Doing a good job and achieving the desired end result are my primary motivation. Whilst I enjoy working on a project on my own, I'm particularly motivated by the buzz of working in a team. It's very rewarding working closely with others who share the same common goal. I like to take on a challenge; I like to rise to that challenge as part of a concerted team effort, and I appreciate it when my boss compliments me for a job well done.

6. Are you proactive?

Alternative and related questions

How good are you at taking the initiative?

The meaning behind the question

Being proactive means making an effort to anticipate a situation and acting in advance either to prepare for it or to prevent it. It's not exactly the same as taking the initiative but the two are certainly closely related.

In asking you this question the interviewer wants to establish what your definition of proactive is and whether or not you are proactive because it is a highly desirable characteristic.

Your answer

This is a prime example of a question requiring you to deliver a specific example whether or not the interviewer actually asks you for one. If you fail to illustrate your answer with an example then it's going to be fairly meaningless. Anyone can claim to be proactive but can you actually prove it?

Choose your example carefully in advance, describe the circumstances to the interviewer and, most importantly, explain what the benefits of your actions were.

EXAMPLE

Yes, I would consider myself to be proactive. I believe it's very important to be as proactive as possible. As the saying goes, a stitch in time saves nine. When my team is working on a project I always do my best to identify possible problems in advance and to make sure that we address them. Recently, a major project of ours was severely affected by a key member of staff leaving the company overnight (for personal reasons). I anticipated that, as a result of this, we wouldn't be able to deliver the solution to the client on time. I took the decision to contact the client, explain the situation, apologise for the delay but make the point that the quality of the finished solution was of greater importance than delivering it on schedule. The client appreciated my honesty, was very understanding and was pleased to hear that we'd never compromise on quality just to be seen to meet a deadline.

7. Are you creative?

Alternative and related questions

In what ways would you say you are creative?

Are you innovative/inventive?

The meaning behind the question

There's no hidden meaning here. It's a very direct question; every walk of life requires at least some degree of creativity, and creativity is often seen as an indicator of intelligence. My core question, 'Are you creative?' is a closed question but answering it with a straight 'Yes' isn't going to get you anywhere. Regardless of precisely how the interviewer phrases their question you need to aim to tell them in what ways you are creative, how this applies to your line of work and to back this up with at least one example.

Your answer

Some lines of work are more creative than others, and the way you phrase your answer will depend on what you do for a living. If you work in a creative field then you will need to give a much more comprehensive answer. But even if you work in a field that isn't generally seen as particularly demanding in terms of creativity, you should be able to come up with an example of where you have displayed lateral or out-of-the-box thinking or invented a new and better way of handling something.

EXAMPLE

Yes, I believe I'm a creative individual. I'm certainly able to think laterally and to be inventive in terms of finding solutions to problems. Quantity surveying isn't generally seen as a particularly creative profession, but I have nevertheless used my creative abilities on numerous occasions; for example, converting old manual systems of reporting to highly automated and much more accurate spreadsheet-based systems. This saved me and my team a considerable amount of time in the long term as well as meaning we were less exposed to the professional embarrassment of errors in our calculations.

8. Are you a risk taker?

Alternative and related questions

How do you feel about taking risks?
Do you have a problem with taking risks?

The meaning behind the question

'Are you a risk taker?' is a very direct question. What the interviewer is really looking for is to assess what your *attitude* is to taking risks. In some lines of work someone who takes risks is definitely going to be a liability. However, in many lines of work the ability to weigh up risks and to take *calculated* risks is an important skill.

Your answer

Your answer will inevitably depend on what the job is that you are applying for. If it is one in which taking risks or cutting corners is likely to be frowned upon then you're going to need to formulate your answer so as to make it clear that you are not someone who believes in risks. You may even want to emphasise that you see it as part of your job to identify potential risks and pre-empt them.

If assessing risks and taking appropriate risks is going to be a feature of your new job then your answer will be very different. You certainly want to avoid the impression of being in any way reckless. Your emphasis should be on the steps you take to identify and gauge risks, only taking risks where you have calculated the potential outcomes and deemed that your actions are going to be worth the risk. You should also make some mention of your decision-making capabilities because being prepared to take calculated risks is, ultimately, a form of decision making.

> ### EXAMPLE
>
> It depends on how you define risk. I am certainly not somebody who takes unnecessary risks, nor risks that would in any way compromise anyone's personal safety. However, I fully appreciate that commercial success is dependent on taking risks – calculated risks. If, having given a matter careful consideration and weighed up the possible ramifications, I determine that a risk is, in the best interests of the business, ▶

worth taking then I am not afraid to take it. You can't always be right, but careful planning and analysis should tip the odds in your favour and ensure that, overall, your decisions pay off. Experience is, of course, essential, and the experience I have gained over the course of my career is invaluable in informing my decisions.

9. How do you handle pressure and stress?

Alternative and related questions

Can you tell me about a time when you were under significant pressure and how you handled that?

Do you thrive under pressure?

How do you cope with the numerous conflicting demands on your time?

What causes you stress at work and why?

The meaning behind the question

The ability to cope with pressure and stress is essential in almost all walks of life, whether you're working checkout at the supermarket or heading up a major corporation. Pressure and stress are unavoidable aspects of the world we live in. The interviewer will be looking to identify:

➤ that you recognise that pressure and stress are facts of life;

➤ that you understand the effect pressure and stress have on you;

➤ that you are sufficiently robust to be able to take them in your stride.

Your answer

Because of the variety of ways in which an interviewer can question you on this topic, it's important that you fully understand what the difference is between pressure and stress because many people use the two terms interchangeably.

Being under pressure is a matter of having significant demands made of you; being challenged to achieve something which is either difficult to achieve in and of itself or difficult to achieve within the time frame that has been set. Pressure is largely a positive force and a motivating factor for many people.

Stress, on the other hand, is not so positive. Stress occurs when the pressure you are under exceeds your ability to effectively meet the demands being made of you. Stress is essentially what an individual experiences when exposed to excessive pressure, and long-term stress can cause all sorts of problems.

I am sure that everyone reading this book has, at some stage in their lives, experienced pressure and stress and knows exactly what they're like.

The key to formulating your answer to this question is to seize this as an opportunity to talk about a situation or an occasion where you were under pressure and how you rose to the challenge. Try to avoid talking about an occasion when you were totally stressed out, but acknowledge that you understand stress and are able to deal with it appropriately.

Avoid conveying the impression that the fact you were under pressure was in any way your own fault or due to your personal failings. Place the blame firmly on external factors outside your control.

Different lines of work are subject to different levels of pressure and stress and this will have a bearing on how you phrase your answer.

EXAMPLE

Working for a small start-up company the past few years has been quite a high-pressure experience on occasion. I've had to deal with numerous conflicting demands on my time and often very limited resources. With careful planning and organisation you can normally reduce the pressure you are under but there will always be factors at play which are outside your control. Personally, while it makes a nice break to have a few pressure-free days, I generally thrive under pressure. I use it to help channel my energies into accomplishing as much as possible. Naturally, there are sometimes occasions when the pressure I'm put under is excessive and this can be stressful. However, I'm sufficiently experienced to appreciate that there is only so much you can reasonably be expected to be capable of and the solution is not to panic, but to remain focused on delivering your very best.

10. Can you tell me about a time when you have failed to achieve a goal?

Alternative and related questions

What's the biggest failure you've experienced in your career?

Can you tell me about a time when you've failed to meet an important deadline?

The meaning behind the question

As well as pinpointing a particular 'failure' in your career, the interviewer will also be gauging your overall attitude to failure, how you deal with adversity. Everyone experiences some failures during the course of their careers, but not everybody bounces back and learns as much from the experience as they perhaps should.

Your answer

You might think this is a tough question because there's no way to answer it without admitting failure. But it's not really that tough. The secret is to avoid picking too major a failure and whatever example you choose, to subtly blame the failure on factors outside your control. You should be very wary indeed of laying the blame at the doorstep of a former boss or colleague; this can backfire on you spectacularly. However, you can certainly dilute some of the blame by saying that you were working as part of a team at the time.

EXAMPLE

In my last job we were given the opportunity to pitch for a major contract at relatively short notice. I was part of a team that spent a couple of weeks working very hard on the tender and it was clear that our company was undoubtedly the best choice for the contract. Unfortunately, the client had employed a rather inexperienced individual to review the tenders and they fell for a competitor's sales pitch, which had a lot less substance but a lot more spin. It was a major blow. I was naturally very disappointed at what seemed a very unfair decision, especially having put so much effort into the tender, but I wrote it down to experience and got on with successfully bidding for other contracts. The following year, the client, having been very dissatisfied with our competitor's performance, asked us to re-tender for the contract. This time we won it. We did, of course, learn some lessons from our previous failure, but most of all we were fortunate that the individual responsible for reviewing the tenders this time was a lot more experienced.

Word of warning

Don't be tempted to say you've never failed. The interviewer won't believe you.

---

11. What's the worst mistake you've made at work and how did you deal with it?

Alternative and related questions

Can you tell me about a time when you made a major error at work?

The meaning behind the question

What the interviewer is trying to extract from you is not an admission of guilt, but a demonstration of how you reacted to your error and what steps you took to resolve it. You can learn a lot about someone from the way they handle their mistakes.

Your answer

As with the previous question, you might think this rather a tough one. The interviewer has specifically asked you about the very worst mistake you've ever made at work. The key is to realise that everyone makes mistakes; the important thing is to learn from them and make sure you never make the same mistake twice.

Also, just because they've asked you what the worst mistake you've made was, that doesn't necessarily mean you have to tell them. Try to talk about a mistake that was clearly severe but is unlikely to put them off hiring you completely. How? By choosing carefully and placing the emphasis on what you did to resolve the situation and what you learned from the experience.

If you can subtly apportion some of the blame to circumstances out of your control, or if you can choose an example which didn't directly involve your work then it's going to strengthen your answer. It also helps if you can pick an example which goes back some way in time. However, you definitely want to avoid coming across as someone who can't admit their own mistakes.

EXAMPLE

I think the worst mistake I ever made at work was in my first-ever job, five years ago. A more senior member of the team seemed to take an instant dislike to me from the start, and one day she was particularly unpleasant to me in front of several colleagues. Later on, I was talking to one of those colleagues who I thought was attempting to console me. Angry and hurt, I foolishly vented my feelings and told her what I thought of the woman in question. I was naturally shocked to find out that my colleague went on to tell everyone what I had said and this certainly didn't help my relationship with the team member who was causing me problems. Rather than let the situation carry on, I chose to have a quiet word with her to find out what her problem was with me and to see if we could put it behind us. It turned out it was nothing personal; she just resented the fact that a friend of hers had also been interviewed for my position and had been turned down. Once we had got matters out into the air, her behaviour changed and we actually got on quite well after that. However, I certainly learned a lot from the experience. I learned that careful communication is vital in managing interpersonal relationships and that if I have a problem with someone it's always best to talk it over with them rather than with someone else.

BLOOPER!

Choose your example carefully. I once had a candidate tell me about the time she 'lost' a leg. She was working as a runner in theatre and the surgeon handed her the limb he had just amputated. She put it down, and, unfortunately, forgot all about it. 'To this day I don't know what happened to that leg,' she reminisced wistfully.

12. How would you handle the following situation?

Alternative and related questions

What would you do if you were presented with the following scenario?

The meaning behind the question

Often, an interviewer may pose a hypothetical scenario-based question telling you to imagine yourself in a difficult or negative situation and asking how you would deal with it.

By confronting you with an unexpected situation and getting you to think on your feet, they can tell a lot about how you would actually react under such circumstances.

Your answer

The answer you should give will depend on the scenario the interviewer outlines. You need to try to identify what their expectations of you would be under the circumstances, and highlight the skills and techniques you would use to deal with the situation.

For the purposes of the example below, please imagine the following scenario:

You are a receptionist working on the front desk when all of a sudden an urgent email arrives, several phone lines start ringing, an important client walks in and a courier turns up with a package that requires your signature. How do you cope with this situation?

In this example, you should be able to identify that the interviewer is probing your ability to prioritise, to 'firefight' and to not panic.

EXAMPLE

My first priority would be to answer the calls whilst simultaneously presenting the waiting clients and the courier with a professional and friendly smile. The calls can be answered and either put straight through or put on hold, allowing me to deal with the client and then the courier thereafter. The people waiting in front of me are able to

▶

see just how busy I am, whereas those on the phone will simply feel ignored if their calls are not answered promptly and may hang up. Having successfully prioritised the calls and the visitors, I would then be able to respond to the email when there is more time.

13. Can you tell me about a major project you have successfully completed?

Alternative and related questions

Can you tell me about a major project that you have recently managed?

The meaning behind the question

The interviewer isn't really interested in the project itself; they're interested in how you successfully completed the project. They're looking for evidence of your ability to successfully complete a project and they're trying to ascertain how your key skills contribute to this ability.

Your answer

The emphasis in this question is on a project that you have *successfully* completed. It's a perfect opportunity to blow your own trumpet.

Make the very most of this question to highlight your skills and abilities which led to the successful completion of the project being careful to pick those which are of most relevance to the job for which you are now applying. Make your contribution to the project clear. What role did you have to play in its success?

Unless the interviewer specifically asks you for a project for which you had sole responsibility, it is reasonable to assume that they are happy with your talking about a project you worked on as part of a team, which is the case for the majority of projects.

It is also best to talk about a project you completed recently. If you go too far back, the interviewer might wonder why you can't cite a more recent example.

EXAMPLE

I was recently involved in organising our participation at a trade fair. It was a major project. We'd never done a trade fair before, but we felt it could be a useful method of drumming up new business. It took a considerable amount of planning and organisation on my part; I had to assess everything that would need to be arranged in advance, from hiring the lighting set-up to liaising with our designers on the production of appropriate corporate literature for us to hand out. I had to make sure I didn't miss the smallest of details; for example, I had to check the plans of our stand to ensure our extension cables were long enough to reach all our equipment. On the day itself, we were on site very early to make sure everything was in place, tested and fully functioning prior to the arrival of the visitors just in case there were any last-minute hitches, which, thankfully, there weren't. The event was very successful and our stand attracted a lot of attention. It was a very busy day. We were able to pitch our services to hundreds of people and pass on their contact details for our sales team to follow up on. Following the success of this event, we're now looking at future events we can attend.

14. Can you tell me about a major problem at work that you've had to deal with?

Alternative and related questions

Can you tell me about a major project you were involved with that went wrong?

The meaning behind the question

Problems are inevitable, no matter what your line of work. The interviewer isn't particularly interested in the problem per se. What they're interested in his how you dealt with it; what action you took and what the outcome of that action was.

Employers don't want problems; they want solutions and they rely on their staff to deliver those solutions. The interviewer wants to make sure that you're just the sort of employee who would be able to do that.

Your answer

This isn't the same question as Question 11, 'What's the worst mistake you've made at work and how did you deal with it?' so make sure you don't give the same answer. It would definitely be a blunder to pick an example of a problem which you yourself had caused, or was caused by a colleague of yours.

You should also avoid picking a problem where a colleague or a member of your staff was the problem. Try to choose a simpler and less controversial topic. The best examples to pick are those where the problem was caused by circumstances beyond your organisation's control.

Since they're referring to a problem in the past, it's important for you to choose an example which not only highlights your problem-solving capabilities but shows them to be relevant to the job for which you are now applying.

EXAMPLE

The weather caused us major problems just a couple of months ago. There was very heavy overnight snowfall, and with all the buses cancelled and only a few trains running, only a few members of our admin team managed to get into work. There was nothing for it but to firefight; we didn't have enough staff to get everything done that would normally need to be done. I established what our main priorities were; what activities were most essential to the running of our department and made sure that we had those covered. I identified less important tasks that we could postpone for a few days until we had the full team back. I also spoke to all the missing team members to see if there were any other urgent priorities of which we, in the office, were unaware. We worked hard and fast right through lunch, and despite feeling that the phone was always ringing, we managed to keep everything running smoothly until things were back to normal.

15. We have a problem with x. How would you resolve that?

Alternative and related questions

Can you tell me about a difficult problem that you resolved?
Can you tell me about a major problem at work that you've had to deal with?

The meaning behind the question

Following on from the previous question, this question is, again, directly probing your problem-solving capabilities, but is doing so in a way that is directly relevant to the job for which you are applying.

The interviewer is trying to identify what you could really bring to the organisation.

They're also assessing how able you are to think on your feet because they'll know there is no way you could have pre-prepared your answer to this one.

Your answer

Problem x could be just about anything. It could be a hypothetical problem but it's probably more likely to be a real-life problem currently facing the prospective employer.

The main difficulty you face with this question is that it's almost impossible to prepare for in advance. You're going to have to think fast. However, rather than replying immediately, I'd suggest you buy some time by getting the interviewer to talk a little more about the problem. Don't be afraid to ask them a few questions to make sure you fully understand what the problem is and what the circumstances are. As well as arming you with more facts, this will also give you some valuable thinking time.

If you're asked the alternative question, 'Can you tell me about a difficult problem that you resolved?' then you're lucky because you can prepare a perfect example for this well in advance of the interview. Please refer to the previous question, Question 14, 'Can you tell me about a major problem at work that you've had to deal with?' for details of how best to handle this.

16. What do you do when you disagree with your line manager?

Alternative and related questions

What would you do if you disagreed with a decision taken by your line manager?

Would you make your opinion known if you disagreed with a decision taken by a superior?

The meaning behind the question

Ostensibly, you might think the interviewer is testing to see how subordinate you are. This isn't really the case. It's not to an organisation's advantage to be filled with people who never question authority or who never voice their opinion. What the interviewer is really looking for is to identify the manner in which you would express your disagreement.

Your answer

A lot depends on what it is that you disagree with. Is it a minor issue which boils down to a matter of your judgement against theirs, or is it a more serious situation which could potentially call for your having to go over their head and discuss the matter with their superior?

You want to avoid talking about the second possibility. Build your answer around the scenario of a minor disagreement and place the emphasis on how you would use your communication and interpersonal skills.

EXAMPLE

Inevitably there will be times when I disagree with my manager's point of view or with a decision she has taken or intends to take. In my current role, my manager welcomes input from her team, and whilst I appreciate that it isn't appropriate to openly disagree with her, I will query issues in private with her as necessary. There may be factors leading to her decision of which I am unaware. Alternatively, once we've both discussed our thoughts, we may simply agree to disagree. I have to respect that it remains her prerogative to make a decision whether I agree with it or not and I must support her in that course of action to the best of my ability.

17. How would you describe yourself as a manager?

Alternative and related questions

What is your management style?
How do you manage people?

The meaning behind the question

There's nothing too complex about this question. The interviewer wants to know what your perception of leadership is and how you go about the day-to-day responsibility of management.

They're only going to be asking this question if you're applying for a management-level role and they're hoping to gauge just how successful you are likely to be in fulfilling such a role.

It's also going to be of interest to them to see how you perceive yourself. It can tell them a lot about you as a person.

Your answer

Unless you really are the perfect manager, try to interpret this question in terms of the manager you aspire to be because that's the kind of manager the interviewer is wanting you to be.

There are two main aspects to a management role:

➤ Getting the job done.
➤ Handling the people who will help you to get the job done.

Your answer needs to cover both these points.

The points you raise in your answer will depend on the kind of management role for which you are applying. Different employers will have different expectations of how their managers should behave and what they are expected to achieve.

> **BLOOPER!**
>
> One candidate, who might well have been a dab hand at delegation, failed to come across well at interview by answering this question with, 'I don't do anything that I can make someone else do for me!'

I'm a very hands-on manager. Whilst I am clearly in charge of my team, we are nonetheless a team and I am a member of that team. When the circumstances require it, I will assert my authority and lead my staff in the direction I have determined we should go. However, I'm always open to ideas and suggestions and consider myself to be very approachable in that respect. I realise the importance of motivating my staff to deliver their best and I'm tactful and diplomatic when dealing with potential problems; I believe a lot more can be achieved through communication than through conflict. I am nevertheless very results-driven and expect every member of my team to pull their weight and help us to achieve our common goals.

18. Can you give me an example of when you have successfully coached a member of your team?

Alternative and related questions

Have you ever been asked to help train a new member of staff?

The meaning behind the question

You'd be wrong in thinking that this is a question just for managers; it could be asked of anyone who works in a team, which is pretty much everyone. In all lines of work the ability to help others to further develop their skills and experience is a valuable attribute. How you describe your example will tell the interviewer a lot about you.

Your answer

You need to structure your answer logically so as to identify what the circumstances were, why the individual needed coaching, how you went about coaching them and, most important of all, what the outcome was. Coaching a team member is a project like any other. In order to deliver a successful answer to this question you're going to need to demonstrate a successful outcome to your efforts.

The example you select will depend on your own personal experiences, but whatever example you choose, make sure you come out of it as the hero of the day.

If you're struggling to find an example then the easiest solution is normally to pick a time when you had to help deal with a new member of staff. 'Coaching' is a very broad term and helping to train a new colleague certainly falls under its umbrella.

EXAMPLE

In my current job for a mail-order company, I work as part of a team, processing orders received and liaising directly with our customers by telephone to handle and resolve any problems or queries. Whilst administration forms the majority of the workload, there's also a lot of customer contact. Recently, my manager took the decision to hire a new team member who had a lot of very valuable customer-facing experience but not so much administrative experience. Whilst the new member of staff needed no help dealing with customers on the telephone, it was obvious from the start that she was struggling with the administrative side of things. As one of the most experienced members of the team, my manager asked if I could take this individual under my wing and help her to resolve the administrative difficulties she was having. Over a period of several days I took the time for her to initially shadow me in the work I was doing before moving on to let her do the work herself under my careful observation. She learned very quickly and within the week she was fully up to scratch and has since become an invaluable member of the team.

---

19. What is your customer service philosophy?

Alternative and related questions

Can you tell me about a difficult client/customer you've had and how you handled them?

Can you give me an example of an occasion when you exceeded a client's/customer's expectations?

The meaning behind the question

Most organisations provide a product or service to a customer. Some definitions of 'customer' are obvious: Marks & Spencer sells sandwiches to the public. Some are less obvious: The Job Centre helps the unemployed return to work.

Customer service skills are important in many different walks of life, and this question is designed to probe your customer service skills. It is more far-reaching than that, though, because many of the same skills which will enable an individual to work well with customers will also help them to work well with their colleagues.

Your answer

However the interviewer phrases their question, the main thrust of your answer should be to outline your customer service skills.

If you can illustrate your answer with an example of when you have delivered outstanding customer service, then so much the better. Outstanding customer service could include resolving a difficult client's complaint or it could be a case of your having exceeded a customer's expectations. Whatever example you select, make sure it is one which shows you in a positive light, i.e. if you want to talk about an unsatisfied client then it had better not be your actions which caused their dissatisfaction.

EXAMPLE

I believe the customer is central to everything we do. Profits are certainly our ultimate goal, but without customer satisfaction, profits will suffer. I attach a lot of importance to customer service. A business is nothing without its customers and it's vital to recognise this. I believe I have strong customer service skills and working with the public is certainly something I enjoy. It's not always easy, of course. Recently, I had to deal with a particularly difficult client who was – fairly unreasonably, it has to be said – very dissatisfied with the solution our sales team had sold them. Rather than let the complaint escalate, I took the time to calmly and patiently listen to the customer and to demonstrate that I understood and empathised with their concerns. This alone took a lot of the wind out of their sails. I went on to give them my viewpoint, addressing their concerns one by one and explaining why I felt the solution they had been sold was the best one for them. It turned out that they had principally misunderstood what was being offered, and once realisation set in, they were actually quite apologetic.

20. How did you get your last job?

Alternative and related questions

How did you locate your last job?

The meaning behind the question

This is a popular question amongst interviewers because whilst seemingly a very simple little question, your answer can give the interviewer insight into numerous different areas. It can help them to assess how much initiative you have, how determined and tenacious you are, how driven you are and how much you plan and control your own career.

Your answer

There are two different ways of interpreting this question and you need to make sure you cover both bases. First of all is the question of how you actually managed to locate your last job (recruitment agency, network contact, speculative application, headhunted etc.). Then there is the question of how you went about securing the job; how you convinced the employer that you were the right person for the job. You need to aim to portray an image of somebody in control of their own destiny, not someone who just goes with the flow.

EXAMPLE

It was actually quite complicated. I was keen for a new challenge and had already started looking around when I saw in the local newspaper that they were opening a new branch in the area. I sent in a speculative application to the HR department at their head office and they wrote back to say that they would only be recruiting through their preferred recruitment agency. So I called them up immediately, and, having run through a few key points on my CV, managed to persuade them to interview me. The company also interviewed a spread of candidates from the recruitment agency but after a second and then a third interview with the marketing director, I was offered the job.

21. What does your current job involve on a day-to-day basis?

Alternative and related questions

Can you describe an average day in your job?

The meaning behind the question

They've read your CV; they know what your job involves. Now they want to hear it straight from the horse's mouth. There's nothing more to their question than that; however, giving the best answer is a little more complicated.

Your answer

As I say, the interviewer has read your CV (or application form), so they know more or less what your job entails. It would definitely be a mistake to answer this question by simply reeling off everything you've stated on your CV. The last thing you want to do is bore the interviewer.

Whilst the description you give on your CV will be comprehensive (and rightly so), when it comes to answering this question you'd do better to skip a lot of the detail and focus on what's really important; what your job is really about. In particular, you want to focus on areas of your current job which most closely match the job for which you are now applying.

Rather than phrasing your work in terms of duties, try to portray what you do in terms of responsibilities.

EXAMPLE

My most important responsibility is to achieve sales. I spend most of my day on the shop floor, talking directly to potential customers and trying to establish their needs. I have a very thorough knowledge of our product range, so if they're unsure of their decision I can give them appropriate advice. I can also steer them towards other, perhaps more expensive product lines that they haven't already considered. By building rapport with the customer and addressing any concerns they may have, I have a good chance of closing the sale. I also aim to up-sell on the till where possible, to maximise the value of each new customer. Amongst other responsibilities I help to control stock levels and liaise with head office accordingly to make sure we are neither overstocked nor understocked. I am also involved in the financial management of the branch, working alongside the branch manager to put together monthly reports etc. Given my level of experience, I am also tasked with helping to bring on board new members of staff, training them in our systems and helping them to maximise their sales potential.

22. What contribution do you make to the department in which you work?

Alternative and related questions

How does your job relate to the overall goals of your department/ organisation?

The meaning behind the question

The interviewer could have rephrased this question, 'Are you able to see the bigger picture?' They're searching for evidence that you understand the purpose and goals of your department as a whole and how your role fits into the big scheme of things. Whilst it might not be vital to your ability to undertake your job, it is always preferable for an employee to understand what the overall purpose is of their team or department and what part they are expected to play in that.

Your answer

Even if the interviewer hasn't phrased their question using the word 'contribution', you still need to place a clear emphasis in your answer on what it is that you contribute to the overall goals of your department. You've got to demonstrate your value. The interviewer knows what job you perform but how is it of benefit to your colleagues and to your employer?

Some people won't necessarily work in a specific department as such; if this is the case for you, then you can simply talk about the contribution you make to other departments and to the organisation as a whole as in the example below.

> **EXAMPLE**
>
> Whilst I am technically part of the IT department, all my colleagues focus very much on keeping the company's computer infrastructure fully functional. As the company's only web developer, I work very much on my own in managing and enhancing the website. I do liaise closely with other departments, though, most particularly marketing and HR. As the website is primarily used as a marketing vehicle and as a way to source new employees, my work is of significant importance to both of these departments. The systems I put in place to collect potential sales leads online make a major contribution to the results of the sales team; these days more and more of our new business comes via the website. And by identifying ways to attract potential new employees online, I have contributed to a reduction in the amount we spend on recruitment consultants, again resulting in a direct impact on the company's bottom line.

23. What changes have you made to your current job role since you started?

Alternative and related questions

How have you changed the job you've been doing?

The meaning behind the question

All job roles evolve over time, some more than others. The interviewer isn't asking how your job has changed since you were first appointed; they're asking how *you* have changed it. They're looking for evidence of initiative, drive and enthusiasm. The best employees are always looking for ways to make improvements; to change things for the better. It's easy for an employee to sit back and just accept things the way they are but that's not the sort of employee who is going to help drive an organisation forward.

Your answer

An interviewer should only be asking this question if your current job is one in which you can reasonably be expected to have made changes to your role.

In many roles there is limited scope for making changes, so your interviewer probably won't be expecting too dramatic an example. If you have been responsible for a tangible improvement to your role then this is obviously going to be an excellent choice. Alternatively, it should be more than sufficient to describe ways in which you took on additional duties and responsibilities that weren't part of your original job description.

Be aware that this is the sort of question that an interviewer is particularly likely to check up on when taking up your references, so it's essential to be absolutely honest.

EXAMPLE

When I first took over the role, I noticed that my predecessor (who was in the job for many years) had been using a number of rather outdated and laborious systems to help them manage the allocation of work to our subcontractors. This was clearly wasting a significant amount of time – and time is money. I, therefore, consulted with my manager and outlined a proposal to scrap these various manual systems and replace them with a single system running on software I had become adept at using in my previous role. Given the low cost of the software and the obvious advantages of my proposal, my manager agreed to the plan. Having spent a couple of weeks setting up the new system, I, consequently, reduced my workload substantially and I was able to use this spare time to help my manager with his financial reporting. This gave me useful additional experience and also freed up my manager to spend more time on other issues.

Word of warning

It can be easy to misunderstand this question and interpret it along the lines of, 'What changes have you made in your current job?' It's easy enough to do as there's really only one word difference between 'to' and 'in', but make no mistake, this is a very different question, and no matter how good your answer to it, your interviewer won't be impressed if you fail to answer the question they actually asked.

So just to make it clear, if they ask: 'What changes have you made *to* your current job role?' they are looking for the answer detailed above. If, on the other hand, you are asked, 'What changes have you made *in* your current job?' they are asking about the things you have achieved, e.g. implementing a new system, reducing headcount, increasing productivity.

24. What have you learned in your last job?

Alternative and related questions

What have you learned in each of your previous roles?

The meaning behind the question

The interviewer could have asked, 'What have you learned in your last job, which will be of use to you in this job?' because that is what they're driving at. They're not asking you to talk about your duties, responsibilities or achievements. They're specifically asking in what ways you have developed professionally whilst working in your last job (or any particular job of their choice).

Your answer

It's vital that your answer should cite one or more examples which are directly relevant to the role for which you are now applying. There's no point in discussing something which isn't going to be of obvious value to you or, more specifically, your employer in your next job.

The chances are that your previous role(s) will have prepared you in various ways to meet the challenge of your next job. Try to ascertain what is likely to be of most interest to the interviewer. What are the key requirements of this vacancy? What have you learned that will ensure you meet those requirements? Select at least one idea, if not two or three, and turn it or them into strong selling points.

There's no need to highlight how this relates to the role you're applying for. It should be self-evident, and if you make a point of it, there is a risk the interviewer might think you're just telling them what they want to hear.

My last job was an excellent learning opportunity and I developed my skills and experience in numerous different ways. Whilst I already had strong IT skills, I didn't have any previous experience of Microsoft Access. When my employer introduced a new order management system which used Access they gave me the opportunity to under-take additional training to be able to work effectively with this. I was then able to put this training into practice on a day-to-day basis and I am now extremely adept at using the package. I also learned a great deal about handling customers. My previous roles were not customer-facing so it was great to have the chance to develop this area of my experience.

25. Can you tell me about your last appraisal?

Alternative and related questions

How was your performance rated in your last appraisal?
How would you comment on your last appraisal?
What areas for improvement were identified at your last appraisal?

The meaning behind the question

Appraisals are supposed to address both your strengths and your weaknesses; both your achievements and your failings. However, the interviewer will know that appraisals focus more on where there is room for improvement than on giving you a pat on the back. This question is a clever ploy to get you to confess precisely where there is room for improvement in your performance.

Your answer

You're going to need to be careful with your answer to this question. For a start, it's very important to be totally honest because the interviewer can easily check up on this sort of information when taking up your references, and if it's an internal vacancy for which you are applying, then you can be more or less sure they will already have examined your last appraisal.

It's not a difficult question to get right. You need to focus on the positive points that were brought up in your last appraisal and only touch briefly on any less positive points, making sure that you confirm these are issues you have now addressed or are in the process of addressing. You're under no obligation to relate every last detail of your last appraisal, so I would vote in favour of mentioning several positive points, but limiting your answer to cover just one weaker point. If your appraisal brought up an apparent weak point that you can put a positive slant on, then so much the better.

Not all employers have a formal appraisal system and this will simplify your answer. It would, however, be a good idea to mention that, whilst there was no formal system in place, you have routinely received positive feedback on your performance, both from your boss and from your colleagues.

EXAMPLE

My last appraisal was very positive. My manager felt that I had made excellent progress in many areas and had really mastered the intricacies of the project we were working on. He did say that he felt other members of the team had become too dependent on me and that a lot of my time was being taken up in showing them how to tackle difficult or unusual issues. Whilst he perceived this as an area for improvement, I perceived this as further evidence that the time is now right for me to take a step up to a management-level position, hence my applying for this role with yourselves.

26. How would you describe your current boss?

Alternative and related questions

What do you think of your current boss?
What kind of a relationship do you have with your current boss?

The meaning behind the question

The interviewer may just be idly curious as to what your current boss is like, but don't count on it. They're much more likely to be probing your perceptions of authority and, in particular, how you handle authority. Whilst seemingly innocuous, this is actually quite a loaded question. If the interviewer identifies you as having any problems with authority then it's going to be a big black mark on your application.

Your answer

This is most certainly not the same question as the tough alternative, 'What are your current boss's weaknesses?' that we cover in the next chapter and you should avoid making any disparaging comments. Regardless of what a loser you might think your boss is, it isn't going to get you anywhere to slate them. Statistically, having problems with their boss is the No. 1 reason people give for changing jobs. However, you'd do well just to give a reasonably complimentary description and portray a positive working relationship between the two of you.

EXAMPLE

I'm fortunate to have a pretty positive working relationship with my boss. She gives me a high degree of latitude to get on with my job, whilst always being there to help me with any unusual or difficult situations; to lend me the benefit of her experience. Like many managers, she's often very busy but she does a good job of closely supervising her team, steering us in the right direction and helping us to achieve the results that are expected of us. I know she appreciates the work I do and this obviously helps to motivate me and encourage me to strive to achieve my very best.

---

27. Why did you leave that job?

Alternative and related questions

Have you ever been made redundant and, if so, why?
Have you ever been fired?

The meaning behind the question

This question is distinct from, 'Why do you wish to leave your current position?' that we covered in the previous chapter in that it's not exploring your current motivators in changing jobs; it's exploring your previous reasons for having left a job.

The interviewer might also be hoping to turn up any skeletons you may have in your cupboard, for example, dismissals.

Your answer

We've already covered the topic of changing jobs in detail in the previous chapter under, 'Why do you wish to leave your current position?' and much of that same advice will apply to this question. However, here I'd like to focus on two special cases: two more negative reasons why you might have left a previous job:

➤ Being made redundant.
➤ Being fired/sacked.

I would immediately like to apologise to any readers who have been made redundant. It is in no way my intention to cause any offence by listing redundancy as a negative reason for leaving a job. I fully appreciate that redundancy is a difficult time and that there's often little justice in an employer's choice of who to make redundant. I empathise entirely. However, my reason for including it in this list is not to suggest you've been made redundant through any fault of your own but because being made redundant may unfortunately be perceived in a negative fashion by a prospective employer; therefore, it is a hurdle you need to deal with.

Redundancy hurts. There are no two ways about it. However, you must conceal any bitterness and resentment you may feel and instead convey to the interviewer that, 'Such is life, these things happen,' it wasn't your fault. It is the position that is redundant, not the individual person. Under no circumstances should you criticise the employer that laid you off. Rather than dwell on negative aspects, you must aim to emphasise any positive outcomes, for example, that it gave you the opportunity to undertake some valuable training or that it meant you were able to move on to a new and better position.

EXAMPLE

Unfortunately, a major client that my department was responsible for supplying, decided to withdraw completely from the UK and close all their branches. It appears they had overreached themselves in deciding to expand beyond the USA. Almost everyone in my department was subsequently made redundant. However, with hindsight, it all worked out very well in the end because I was able to secure a new and more senior position within just a couple of months.

If you've been fired from a previous role then this is a tough one to deal with; it's hard to put a positive slant on such matters.

There are two points I need to make about how you should handle this. Firstly, you must be truthful; it's easy for a prospective employer to check these sorts of detail. Secondly, you must convey the circumstances as calmly and dispassionately as possible, acknowledge responsibility for the causes of your dismissal and, above all else, convince the interviewer that you learned a great deal from the experience and that this will never, ever happen again.

There are various words and expressions which can be used to describe being dismissed from a job: 'sacked', 'fired' etc. However, these have more negative connotations than simply saying you were dismissed. Therefore, you should avoid using them in your answer.

EXAMPLE

I was only in that job for a couple of months and I unfortunately left it sooner than I would have liked to. I had an initial probationary period of three months, and during that time I, regrettably, had an argument with a customer. I felt they were being extremely unreasonable, and rather than pacifying them, I let the situation escalate. It turned out that they were a long-standing customer and they used their influence to insist that my manager dismiss me. I was young and inexperienced and I learnt a great deal from it. I would certainly never now argue with a customer; I know that there are much better ways to resolve such a situation.

BLOOPER!

It's probably a good idea to avoid the following answer given by one candidate: 'The company made me a scapegoat, just like my three previous employers.'

28. Which of your jobs was the best?

Alternative and related questions

What's the best job you have ever had?
Can you describe the best job you have ever had?
How would you define your dream job?
In which job were you the happiest/most fulfilled?

The meaning behind the question

This is potentially a trick question. Does the interviewer really care which the best job was? Or are they more interested in identifying what your conception of the perfect job is and how that matches or differs from the vacancy for which they are currently interviewing you? It's much more likely to be the latter. By identifying what you have most enjoyed in the past they can assess how likely you are to enjoy this job in the future.

Your answer

You should endeavour to pick a job which is not greatly dissimilar from the one for which you are applying. You then need to explain your choice in such a way as to emphasise the similarities between that role and this current vacancy, subtly of course.

EXAMPLE

I have tried to plan my career path carefully, only changing jobs when the right role has presented itself. However, I would say my best-ever job was my role with Elisabeth Elkins Catering. I was given a considerable degree of autonomy to conceive, plan and implement our marketing strategy. I had a highly productive working relationship with the managing director and the outcome was very successful; our sales more than tripled by the end of my two years.

Word of warning

Avoid citing your current job. The interviewer will wonder:

➤ if it's that great then why do you really want to leave;

➤ if they do give you this job, is there a risk you might later regret it?

29. Why is there a gap in your CV?

Alternative and related questions

What did you do during this gap in your employment?
Can you tell me more about this break in your career history?

The meaning behind the question

There are two elements here:

➤ The interviewer will be interested in the reasons for there being a gap in your CV; why you experienced a period of unemployment.

➤ They will be interested in what you did during that period of unemployment.

Your answer

Most people have a gap or two in their career history. It's very common and not normally anything to worry about. There is, however, only one explanation that an employer is really going to view favourably:

➤ further training/education.

Other common and conceivably constructive reasons include:

➤ raising a child;

➤ caring for another dependant;

➤ travel.

But there are also reasons which will definitely be viewed negatively:

➤ inability to find a suitable position;

➤ ill health.

If the reason for the gap in your career history isn't obviously negative then there shouldn't be a gap in your CV; you should have included a brief entry explaining the situation. This will prevent an interviewer from asking you, 'Why is there a gap in your CV?' and will instead prompt them to ask the more positive question, 'Can you tell me more about this break in your career history?'

Further training/education: This is very simple and should already be covered within your CV but maybe the interviewer has missed it. You need to politely draw their attention to the further training/education you undertook and use this as an opportunity to talk about why you chose this option and how it adds value to your application.

Raising a child/Caring for another dependant: If you took time out of your career in order to care for a family member or close friend then it is very much your own private affair but one that an interviewer should hopefully view favourably. You should have included a brief entry in your CV explaining the circumstances and the interviewer should refrain from probing too deeply into the matter. The same applies for time out to raise your own family.

Travel: Taking a sabbatical to go travelling is often seen by an employer as a positive thing. Many will believe that the cultural awareness and sense of independence you will have gained as a result of the experience will prove to be of value to them. Also, if you've already taken time out to travel then it means you're less likely to suddenly disappear to travel the world just as they've got you settled in. This is a common worry amongst employers, particularly when it comes to younger employees. If you're questioned on this then it is important to emphasise that it was something you 'needed to do' and now you've 'got it out of your system'. You may also be able to make reference to any temporary and part-time work you undertook in other countries if that could be an additional selling point for you.

Inability to find a suitable position: This is definitely the most common cause for there being a gap in a CV. The problem you face is that if you tell an interviewer you were struggling to find work then that's inevitably going to worry them. You need to deal with this by explaining carefully that the right job isn't always available at the right time. For further advice on how to handle this, please take a look at Question 13, 'You've been out of work for a while, has it been difficult finding a job?' in the next chapter.

Ill health: If you have been absent from work as a result of a significant illness or a major accident, then the interviewer should appreciate that these things do happen. For further advice on how to handle questions about your health please take a look at Question 14, 'What's your sickness record like?' in the next chapter.

30. What do you know about us as an organisation?

Alternative and related questions

What is your impression of our organisation?
Why do you want to work for this organisation?

The meaning behind the question

The interviewer wants to make sure you've done your homework, that you really understand what their organisation is all about and that you have a realistic expectation of what it would be like to work for such an organisation. Whilst they're not going to be deliberately fishing for compliments they will want to ensure that you do have a positive impression of their organisation. Why do you want to work for them in particular?

Your answer

In the previous chapter we covered the closely related question, 'Why do you want to work for this organisation?' The difference with this question is the greater emphasis you need to place on what you know about the organisation rather than why you want to work for their organisation in particular.

Spell out to the interviewer the key points you know about their organisation and how you come to know this, for example, because you've researched their website, or you've read about them in the newspaper etc. But don't go into excessive detail.

Make sure you put a positive spin on any points you raise, and, if at all possible, communicate how you feel you are well suited to working for such an organisation.

Avoid saying anything negative or bringing up any bad press etc. that the organisation may have had.

I've done some research into your organisation to ensure that I fully understand what kind of organisation I would be working for. I read on your website that your sales levels have grown at an average of 25 per cent year on year for the past five years and that you are now working on your expansion into the United States. You're clearly a very progressive organisation and that's exactly what I'm looking for. I want to work for an organisation which doesn't stand still, which is expanding and taking on new and interesting challenges. I've also read a lot of customer comments on various third-party websites and the quality of your service is very impressive.

31. What do you know about our products/services?

Alternative and related questions

Have you ever bought our products/used our services?

The meaning behind the question

The interviewer is again testing to see how interested you really are in the vacancy as defined by the amount of time you have spent researching their operation. Some roles will require greater product/service knowledge than others, and if you are applying for a role where such knowledge is critical, for example, sales, then the question will take on another dimension. If you can't prove you fully understand their product/service then how can you hope to be able to sell it?

Your answer

If you've prepared properly for your interview then you should be able to demonstrate a reasonably in-depth understanding of the organisation's products/services. The degree to which this will be important will depend on your specific line of work. As well as conveying basic facts, it is also a good idea to provide a gentle critique. Whilst you should aim to be more complimentary than critical, if you are able to identify areas for improvement; ideally areas which you yourself would be able to improve, then it is likely to impress the interviewer and count very much in your favour. The best employees rarely accept the status quo; they are always looking for ways to improve things.

I've actually got one of your posters framed on the wall at home. I was already familiar with the range you offer, and since seeing this vacancy advertised, I have had a closer and more detailed look. I'm impressed by what I've seen. They're printed to a high degree of quality, something which isn't always the case with posters produced by other companies, and yet they remain very reasonably priced. Whilst you certainly have many interesting and commercially appealing designs, I do feel that some parts of the range are becoming a little dated. I would certainly welcome the challenge not only of revamping existing designs within the range but also of further developing the range in new and interesting directions.

32. What do you think are our organisation's greatest strengths, weaknesses, opportunities and threats?

Alternative and related questions

What do you think is the greatest advantage we have over the competition?

The meaning behind the question

This is a complex question. The interviewer wants to really put your knowledge of their organisation and of the market in general to the test. Their secondary objective will be to see how you handle a question in four parts – strengths, weaknesses, opportunities and threats. Questions which are really three or four questions in one are often considered to be good basic indicators of intelligence; showing how well your brain can absorb, hold and process multiple concepts simultaneously. Trust me this is not an easy question, especially when you are already under pressure.

FIFTY MORE CLASSIC QUESTIONS: BE PREPARED

Your answer

Fear not. Tricky as this question is, if you've prepared for it (which, if you're reading this, you hopefully will have done) then it all boils down to keeping your cool, breaking the question down into its component parts and addressing each of them in turn, one by one. You should also aim to go heavy on the strengths and opportunities and a little more gently with the weaknesses and threats. It's a big question but try to keep your answer reasonably concise. As with other questions about potentially negative issues, try to put a positive spin on matters. If the role you are being interviewed for could play a part in tackling these weaknesses and threats, then make sure you say so.

EXAMPLE

I think your greatest strengths are your market-leading position and the customer service philosophy which has resulted in this. Every business has its weakness and I think we'd agree that your greatest weakness is the lack of a comprehensive marketing strategy. As we've already discussed, you focus on a few key marketing avenues and are leaving a lot of money on the table in certain other areas. I firmly believe this is something I can help you with and that the development of a broad and consistent marketing strategy is consequently also your greatest opportunity. I also reckon that expanding internationally represents another major opportunity. As for threats, the greatest threat is quite simply the competition. It's vitally important for you to continue to stay one step ahead of them.

---

33. What do you know about the vacancy for which you are applying?

Alternative and related questions

Why have you applied for this vacancy?
What appeals to you most about this vacancy?

The meaning behind the question

The interviewer wants to make sure you really understand the role for which you are applying, and that you fully appreciate what would be involved if you were to be appointed to the role. If they haven't questioned you separately about this then they will also be trying to glean why it is that you applied for this vacancy and why it appeals to you.

Your answer

If you don't have a reasonably thorough understanding of the role (from the job description or person specification etc.), then you shouldn't even be at the interview. You need to demonstrate comprehensively to the interviewer that you fully appreciate what the role entails, and, ideally, you want to try to pre-empt the next question in this chapter, Question 34, 'How do your skills and experience match the job description/person specification?'

For advice on how to deal with explaining why it is that you have applied for this vacancy and why it appeals to you, please refer to the separate questions, 'Why have you applied for this vacancy?' in the previous chapter and 'What appeals to you most about this vacancy?' – Question 35 below.

EXAMPLE

I've carefully studied both the job description and the person specification so I believe I'm fully aware of the precise duties and responsibilities the role entails. You've also helped to clarify a few points during the course of this interview.

You can then go on to deliver your prepared answer to the following question.

34. How do your skills and experience match the job description/person specification?

Alternative and related questions

Do you feel your skills and experience match the job description/person specification?

Do you feel that you have the skills and experience necessary to undertake this job?

The meaning behind the question

Answering this question is going to be one of your interviewer's primary goals. Many of the other questions will lead them towards an answer, but sometimes the interviewer will just come out and ask you directly to tell them how you match the job description/person specification.

As well as helping to gauge how well your skills and experience match what they're looking for, this question will normally also reveal a lot about *how* you perceive the job in question.

Your answer

You're not going to get away with answering, 'Very well!' to this question. What the interviewer expects you to do, and what you very much need to do is to explain precisely *how* your skills and experience match the job description/person specification.

Job descriptions and person specifications are often very lengthy and comprehensive. You don't want to go into too much detail when answering this question – not least because it could get rather boring. The best strategy to adopt is for you to select a handful of issues and briefly talk about each in turn, expressing each in terms of your prospective employer's needs.

You will need to give this some thought and to have determined in advance what skills and experience the interviewer is going to be most interested in.

> **EXAMPLE**
>
> I believe my skills and experience is a very good match for the person specification. You're looking for someone with a significant amount of high-level experience in the retail clothing sector. I now have 25 years' experience within this sector, most recently as general manager of a flagship central London store. You need someone with considerable skill in financial management, able to build turnover, and, most importantly, to build turnover profitably. In my current role my branch now has an annual turnover of £5 million – 40 per cent higher than when I took over the role three years ago. Our profit margin has also grown from 10 per cent to 15 per cent, meaning that profits have more than doubled in just the last three years. The role demands an individual who is adept at managing and leading a large team; I'm currently responsible for 65 retail staff. The role also requires an individual who is able to build profitable long-term relationships with key high-value clients. Successfully catering to the needs of VIP clients is essential to my current role and certainly an aspect that I very much enjoy. Overall, I feel I'm a very good match for the job but would of course be delighted to discuss any particular points in greater detail if you wish.

This answer has obviously been written from the point of view of someone seeking a very senior role. However, the basic principles can easily be adapted to your own specific circumstances. Remember that my examples are purely intended to help illustrate the points made; it's essential for you to think for yourself and to create your own answers.

35. What appeals to you most about this vacancy?

Alternative and related questions

What are you most looking forward to in this job?
What is it that you are looking for in a new job?
Why have you applied for this vacancy?

The meaning behind the question

This question is similar to the top 10 question, 'Why have you applied for this vacancy?' that we discussed in the previous chapter. However, it is sufficiently different – and sufficiently popular – to warrant us covering it separately.

The interviewer knows that there will be a number of factors which drew you to this vacancy. What they are looking for with this question is to identify your key motivator; what really matters most to you. This will give them some insight into you as both a professional and a person.

Your answer

There's a right way and a wrong way to answer this question. The wrong way is to see matters entirely from your own point of view and to cite some aspect of the vacancy which meets your own needs first and foremost. The right way is to make sure you identify some aspect of the vacancy which you can talk about in such a way as to place emphasis on how you meet the organisation's needs. The interviewer is more interested in how you meet their needs than on how they can meet yours.

EXAMPLE

I'm particularly taken by the importance you place on customer service. In too many organisations customer service is very much a secondary priority, whereas you place the customer at the centre of everything you do. As a customer service manager, I am naturally very committed to excellence in customer service, and I am very keen to work with an organisation that attaches the same importance to customer service that I do. A business is nothing without its customers; it's vital to recognise this and your reputation for customer service is enviable. It sets you apart from the competition.

36. Why have you chosen this line of work?

Alternative and related questions

What took you into this line of work?
What do you like best about this line of work?

The meaning behind the question

The interviewer could have asked, 'Was it the right choice?' because this is what they are trying to establish; was this the right choice for you and, if so, why? As with almost every other question they'll be looking for ways in which your answer can be applied to the requirements of the job for which you are applying.

Your answer

Hopefully you've already gone a long way towards convincing the interviewer that you want this job. Now you need to convince them that this line of work really is the right one for you; in what ways are you best suited to it?

You definitely need to demonstrate enthusiasm for your work, and if you can demonstrate passion then that's even better. Above all, you need to show an interest in your line of work and give sound reasons for your having embarked upon this particular career path. Avoid at all costs giving the impression that it is something you just randomly drifted into.

Try to sprinkle your explanation with specific examples of relevant skills and abilities.

EXAMPLE

Both my parents are accountants, so I grew up listening to them talking about their work and I was always very interested in their working lives. Whilst I considered a range of other options, I've always had a particular talent for mathematics, and accountancy was evidently the best choice. I enjoy working with figures; I enjoy applying my mathematical abilities to real-world problems. I also enjoy working with others and I find it very rewarding to get to grips with a client's precise circumstances and to then help them to find the best solutions to the financial problems they are facing. Accountancy was without doubt the right choice for me.

37. Are there any other organisations to which you are applying?

Alternative and related questions

What other organisations are you applying to?
What other jobs have you applied for?
Have you had any other interviews yet?
Have you received any job offers yet?

The meaning behind the question

This question has nothing directly to do with your ability to do the job. The interviewer is trying to gauge how important this particular application is to you and how much you are in demand with other, possibly competing organisations. They want to assess how discerning you are or how desperate you are. If you've already received a firm offer from another organisation then they will know they need to act fast if they don't want to lose you.

Your answer

You've got to tread carefully here. You don't want to be trapped into disclosing too much detail, especially the names of specific organisations. The only exception to this is if you are also applying to a direct competitor. It's a risky move; the interviewer might see this as rather mercenary on your part but it can motivate them to want to secure your services rather than let 'the enemy' take advantage of you. Generally, it's best to dodge the question and give an appropriately vague answer, but above all, to be truthful. If you round off your answer by emphasising that this particular vacancy is your preferred choice, then the interviewer is unlikely to press you for further details of your other applications.

> **EXAMPLE**
>
> Finding the right position is obviously very important to me so I am being rather thorough in my job search. I have been quite selective, but I have identified a number of different jobs and organisations which fit my criteria and my applications for these vacancies have reached varying stages. However, the opportunity with your

company remains my preferred choice both because of the specifics of the role and because the organisation itself is one I feel to be particularly appropriate to me.

38. How does this job compare to others for which you are applying?

Alternative and related questions

Why do you want this particular job?
What most attracts you to this opportunity rather than other vacancies you have applied for?

The meaning behind the question

This is clearly a more probing question than the previous question and you may well find it being asked as a follow-up to this question. The interviewer is trying to gauge how motivated you are to win this particular role as opposed to one of the others currently open to you. They want to know where they fit on the scale.

Your answer

You're going to have to tread a fine line here. It's vital to communicate that this job is, of course, your preferred choice (even if one of the other offers is blatantly superior). However, you most certainly don't want to give the impression that this job is your *only* choice. That would severely weaken your position. The best strategy is to sidestep the question as best you can and focus on the vacancy at hand and what most attracts you to this job and to this organisation.

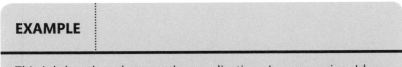

EXAMPLE

This job has the edge on other applications I am pursuing. I have taken my time to identify a number of possibilities which are closely suited to me so as not to waste my time or anyone else's. They all

▶

have various pros and cons, but I am particularly attracted to this job because I feel it offers the best opportunities for me to develop professionally and make a major contribution. It's a perfect match for my skills and experience. I also believe I will fit in very well with the organisation as a whole.

39. Can you describe your ideal employer to me?

Alternative and related questions

Which of your employers was the best?

The meaning behind the question

By identifying what you perceive as the perfect employer, the interviewer can assess how closely their organisation fits this profile and hence how well you are likely to fit in with their organisation. It's a clever question and sets a trap that a weaker candidate is likely to walk straight into. If they don't fit your definition of the ideal employer then why would they want to hire you?

Your answer

It doesn't really matter what your idea of an ideal employer is. What matters is that your description should match the organisation to which you are now applying. Of course, if there's a big difference between your prospective employer and your conception of the ideal employer, then you should perhaps be asking yourself whether this is really going to be the right job for you.

The easiest way to tackle this question is to first identify what it is that you like best about the prospective employer, then build your description of your 'ideal' employer around this.

If you've already prepared an answer to, 'Why do you want to work for this organisation?' (which I covered in the previous chapter), then you can recycle some of the ideas you had for this.

EXAMPLE

My ideal employer would be a large yet growing company with a strong reputation within its sector, a company which offers plenty of scope for progression within the hierarchy. Whilst my preference is for a larger organisation, I want to work for a company which nevertheless has a dynamic and progressive approach. Your organisation certainly more than meets those requirements.

Word of warning

It would be inappropriate to openly state that you feel their organisation to be the 'perfect' employer. You will inevitably come across as phoney.

40. What sort of person would you most like to work for?

Alternative and related questions

Can you tell me about the best boss you've ever had?
Putting yourself in your manager's shoes, what is the best way to manage you?

The meaning behind the question

Along the same lines as the previous question, the interviewer is looking to identify how well you are likely to fit in with your manager. If your prospective manager differs significantly from the description you give, then it's going to raise questions in the interviewer's mind as to how well you are likely to be able to work together.

You should also be aware that the way you answer this question can reveal a lot about what sort of a person you will be to manage.

Your answer

It's best to avoid going into too much detail and giving too precise a description. Try to keep your answer broad so that it is unlikely to exclude too many people. Horoscopes are carefully written so as to sound meaningful and yet remain as vague as possible so that they can be seen to be pertinent by as many people as possible. You want to adopt the same tactic.

By phrasing your answer carefully, you can also score a few discreet points with regard to what sort of a person you are like to work with. Try to convey the impression that you'd most like to work for someone who was a lot like you and then give a positive description of that person.

EXAMPLE

I'd most like to work for someone who has the same approach as I do to getting things done – planning, organisation and action. Also, I'm always keen to take on new duties and responsibilities so I'd welcome a manager who was prepared to give me the chance to continue my professional development. Besides this, a good manager is, of course, always approachable supportive and sensitive to the needs of their team; whilst I'm good at working on my own initiative, every team needs a leader to give it direction.

---

41. In what ways is your degree relevant to the work you are now doing?

Alternative and related questions

Why did you choose to study x at university and how do you feel it is relevant to this job?
What did you learn at university that will help you to undertake this job?

The meaning behind the question

Completing a degree course is a significant undertaking. In asking this question the interviewer is trying to appreciate what your degree course involved and how the skills and experience gained during your time at university will be of use in the job for which you are now applying.

Your answer

The way you answer this question will depend on your circumstances, but there are two main possibilities.

If your degree is directly relevant to the work you are now doing, for example, if you're a doctor, then this question is reasonably straightforward to answer. You just need to pick a few key aspects of your degree course which you have found to be particularly useful to you in your working life. Describe these briefly and demonstrate the bearing they have on your suitability for the role for which you are applying.

If, however, your degree was in criminology and you are now working as a finance assistant, then talking about the module on criminal justice in modern Britain is obviously going to be completely irrelevant. Instead, in such cases, you should be concentrating on:

➤ what transferable skills and abilities you developed during your degree course;

➤ how these skills and abilities relate to your current line of work;

➤ how the experience of completing a degree course has helped you develop as an individual.

Many employers are sceptical as to the real-world value of some degree courses. There is a common perception that graduates lack initiative and the ability to apply their theoretical knowledge to practical purposes. Make sure you dispel any doubts the interviewer may have in this respect.

EXAMPLE

Whilst my degree in geography is of course not directly relevant to my current role as a market researcher, it was nevertheless a very worthwhile experience in many different ways. I developed a broad set of transferable skills, including how to compile, interpret and analyse data; skills I now apply on a daily basis. I also undertook a number of team projects, working together to achieve a goal, including writing up the results of our findings and how best to structure and communicate our arguments. Undertaking a degree course was a major personal challenge and I definitely matured significantly during my time at university; learning how to plan and organise my own workload so as to meet all my deadlines. I feel it has definitely helped to prepare me for my current career.

42. What have you learned and how have you developed over the last year/five years?

Alternative and related questions

What have you learned in your last job?
What have you learned in each of your previous roles?

The meaning behind the question

Ongoing personal and professional development is vital in many different lines of work. The interviewer will be looking for:

➤ evidence that you are someone who takes your continuing development seriously;

➤ details of how you have developed in ways which will be useful to your next job.

Your answer

This question is similar to Question 24, 'What have you learned in your last job?' but is sufficiently different for us to handle it separately. Yes, the interviewer will be interested in what you have learned in your last job but this is a broader question and requires a broader answer, particularly if the interviewer has asked about the past five years instead of just the last 12 months.

You may have developed in numerous ways during the past five years, but you should endeavour to select examples which are directly relevant to the role for which you are now applying. Talk about general ways in which you've developed as an individual, talk about specific training you have undertaken and, above all, make it clear that you have been the driving force behind your development, not your employers.

EXAMPLE

Over the course of the past five years, I have made an effort to develop my skills and experience in numerous different ways. I have matured as an individual and my experience of working with both colleagues and customers has contributed a lot to my interpersonal skills. I am also better able to see the bigger picture and how my role relates to the overall goals of the organisation. Having built up a broad range of experience, I am now much more productive in my role and much better equipped to handle unusual or difficult situations. In terms of training, I have learned a range of new IT skills, including Microsoft PowerPoint and Microsoft Access. I have also undertaken an evening course in business administration, which has helped to shape the way I work and has given a formal structure to many of the skills I was already developing on a practical basis. I am also now a qualified first aider.

43. What sports are you/have you been involved in?

Alternative and related questions

Do you play any sports?

The meaning behind the question

It's hard to say what the interviewer's precise motivations are in asking you this question. There are a number of possibilities; it depends on the interviewer. All interviewers will be looking for evidence that you are a fit and physically active individual. Some will also be looking to gauge whether or not you are a team player or even a team leader. And others will be trying to identify a competitive streak. However, there's actually no evidence that individuals who play sports are any more competitive or any more likely to work well in a team than those who never go near a pair of trainers.

Your answer

If you are involved in any sports then it should already be on your CV, which means the interviewer should know this. In asking you this question, they're expecting you to elaborate on what you've stated on your CV.

If, like many of us, you rarely find time to engage in any sporting activity, then there's no need to fear. This question is unlikely to be a deciding factor in whether or not you get the job. Stick to the truth and try to mention at least one physical activity, even if it's just walking in the park at the weekend.

There's currently little routine to my life. Business needs are such that I travel very frequently and work irregular hours. This leaves little room for me to participate in any sporting activities. However, I do like to keep myself fit and healthy, and I take the opportunity to go for a walk in the morning before I start work, whenever possible. This helps to wake me up, get some oxygen into my brain and I also use the time to think through the day ahead of me and what it is that I need to achieve. I'm aware that there's a lot less travel involved in this job so this means I may have more opportunity in the future to play tennis again.

44. Do you know what the current headline news is?

Alternative and related questions

What news story has interested you recently?

The meaning behind the question

Apart from a handful of professions, for example, journalism, this question is likely to have precious little to do with your ability to perform the job unless it's your particular industry or line of work that's been in the news. Instead, the question is more about the interviewer trying to understand what sort of a person you are; how much active interest you take in the world around you and the society you live in. This gives the interviewer greater insight into your character and helps them to assess how well you will fit in with your prospective future colleagues and with their organisational culture. The interviewer might also want to get your opinion on the matter so as to test your analytical skills.

Your answer

'No' is not an option. Whether or not you're interested in current affairs you need to make sure you're reasonably clued up on what's going on in the world whenever you're sitting interviews. It's a simple enough matter to buy a daily newspaper (avoiding the tabloids) or to watch the news on television. Avoid being controversial; avoid saying too much; volunteer a brief opinion on the matter if appropriate to do so. As well as this being a 'formal' question that might come up at interview, the interviewer could easily make reference to some newsworthy topic in the 'small talk' phase before or, indeed, after an interview. If you haven't got the faintest idea what they're talking about then it's not going to make a good impression.

EXAMPLE

I like to keep abreast of current affairs mainly via the BBC News website, which gives me a thorough, but balanced overview. The major news at the moment remains the ongoing conflict in the Middle East. It's a tragic situation and it's very hard to see what the long-term solution is going to be, so deep-rooted are the problems.

45. How quickly can you adapt to a new work environment?

Alternative and related questions

How long does it generally take you to settle into a new environment? How long do you feel it will take you to make an impact in your new job?

The meaning behind the question

Whenever someone takes up a new role it will inevitably take them some time to settle in. If you've been in your previous job for a number of years then it can be quite a shock to the system starting a new job; you'd be surprised how many employees walk out within their first week. The interviewer isn't necessarily asking you for a precise timescale as to how long you'll take to settle in. What they really want from you is evidence that you understand the upheaval involved in changing jobs and that you are prepared for this and will, consequently, adapt to your new situation as quickly as possible.

Your answer

Above all, you must convey to the interviewer that you are able to adapt quickly to new circumstances. However, more than that, you should attempt to convey why you will be able to adapt quickly to new circumstances. It's all very well to say that you will adapt quickly, but it doesn't mean very much unless you can back up your statement with some convincing evidence.

The best way to handle this is to refer to your current or previous job and how quickly you were able to settle in there.

If this is your first job then you could instead refer to how you handled the start of your degree course or how you settled into your last school.

EXAMPLE

I believe I'm very good at adapting to changes in my circumstances. Whilst every organisation is different and no two jobs I've had have ever been the same, the core requirements of my role don't change. I appreciate that there will inevitably be new procedures that I need to absorb and adhere to, and it also takes time to forge positive working relationships with new colleagues. However, I don't anticipate it taking very long at all before I'm fully up to speed and making a major contribution. When I took up my current role, I'd been with my previous employers for more than five years. It was clearly a major change for me. I nevertheless settled in very quickly, got to know my colleagues and to understand the way the organisation worked, and I already felt quite at home before the end of my first month.

---

46. Would it be a problem if we asked you to work overtime/evenings/weekends?

Alternative and related questions

Would it be a problem for you taking work home occasionally at the weekend?

Do you have a preference for working regular days and hours?

How do you feel about the amount of overtime this role demands?

The meaning behind the question

In some jobs it is going to be essential for you to work unusual hours and if that's the case the interviewer probably wouldn't even be asking you the question. In other lines of work there will be an unspoken expectation that you will be prepared to put in longer hours than the average. Generally, an interviewer is most likely to be asking you this question if working overtime/evenings/weekends isn't the norm for your job. They want to identify how flexible you are in terms of accommodating their needs even when it might be to your own detriment, in other words, how committed you are to your work.

Your answer

It is, of course, entirely up to you how you feel about working above and beyond 'normal' office hours. There will be numerous factors you have to weigh up and the decision is yours alone.

Once you have established your position on the matter, honesty is very much the best policy. Unfortunately, it may well count against you if you're unwilling or unable to work long hours. But don't let yourself be talked into accepting working conditions which you know you won't be happy with unless you really are prepared to live up to your promises.

Whatever your stance, try to communicate your opinion in as reasonable and positive a manner as possible. Even if you aren't keen on overtime, you might be prepared to offer a compromise as in the example below.

EXAMPLE

I'm reasonably flexible and if business needs are such that it would be advantageous for me to work longer hours – and even weekends – then, depending on my other commitments, I would certainly be prepared to do so. However, I would hope that this would be the exception rather than the rule. I do believe in a life outside work, and whilst my job is clearly very important to me, I would generally like to keep my working hours within normal bounds. In my current role I have had to put in some overtime during especially busy periods and I have had no objections to doing so. However, I am efficient and productive and I generally manage to complete my work without having to resort to overtime.

47. What is your current salary package?

Alternative and related questions

How much are you currently earning?

The meaning behind the question

Very simple. The interviewer wants to establish what level of remuneration you currently enjoy and see how that compares to the package their organisation is planning to offer (which may or not have been previously disclosed).

Your answer

Your answer is also very simple. I would strongly recommend against any answer other than the absolute truth. They're not asking what salary package you are expecting for this role (that's the next question in this chapter). They're asking what you currently receive and that's what you need to tell them, although it's always a good idea to emphasise that money is not your only motivator. When it comes to talking money, you never want to come across as mercenary. (The only exception to this would be for those working in sales and other money-driven and largely commission-based roles.)

> **EXAMPLE**
>
> I currently have a basic salary of £32,200 with a Ford Mondeo company car. I also receive an annual bonus; this year it was £2,500. Whilst my remuneration is clearly important, it's most certainly not the only deciding factor in my choice of a new job and a new employer. Continuing my professional development within a suitably challenging role is also very important to me.

48. What salary package are you expecting for this role?

Alternative and related questions

What would you consider to be an appropriate rate of remuneration for this job?

The meaning behind the question

There's nothing complicated about this. Regardless of what you're currently earning, the interviewer wants to identify what it is that you want in order to work for their organisation and to assess how that fits in with what they're prepared to offer.

Your answer

This is not nearly so simple to answer as the previous question. You need to have thought through very carefully both what salary package you can reasonably expect and also what the minimum is that you would be prepared to accept, assuming the job itself was suitably attractive. These are issues only you can decide but it will certainly help to have an awareness of what your 'market value' is. This will take a little research. But that's not to say you should give a precise answer. Unless you have a firm job offer in hand, it's best to dodge the question slightly and quote a range of possibilities.

EXAMPLE

The opportunities I'm currently pursuing generally involve salary packages between £35k and £40k and I am comfortable with this range. Whilst the salary on offer won't necessarily be the deciding factor in my choice, I am keen to achieve a position which offers nearer the high end of this scale; a package which best reflects my worth.

49. When would you be available to start?

Alternative and related questions

What notice period does your current contract stipulate?

The meaning behind the question

Sorry, this doesn't necessarily indicate that you've won the job. The interviewer is generally just planning ahead and trying to identify when, if they were to offer you the job, you would be able to start work. It's a simple, factual question.

Your answer

Your answer is going to be relatively straightforward. Stick to the facts. Tell the interviewer what your current notice period is and how many leave days you remain entitled to since these could reduce your notice period. You should also have decided in advance whether you wish to take advantage of the break between jobs to have a week or two of holiday.

Bear in mind that if the interviewer urgently needs to fill the vacancy then the time frame within which you are able to start may be a deciding factor.

However, most employers are generally very understanding of notice periods and will be prepared to wait if it means they secure the best candidate for the job.

In some circumstances you may even wish to give your current employer more time to replace you than is stipulated in your contract. Whilst this might be inconvenient for your next employer, they may well be impressed by your loyalty and dedication. This should be negotiable anyway, and, if it does pose a major problem for the prospective employer, they will tell you.

EXAMPLE

My current contract stipulates a notice period of four weeks but I have 10 days' leave available to me which effectively reduces my notice period to just two weeks. On receipt of a firm job offer I would intend to resign immediately from my current position and conceivably start my new role just two weeks later.

50. Do you mind if we contact your current employer for a reference?

Alternative and related questions

Would you give us permission to take up appropriate personal and professional references?

The meaning behind the question

Whilst the interviewer's interest in checking your references is certainly not a negative sign, it's still not yet a job offer. Most employers (if they have any sense) will take up references before hiring someone. It's always a sensible precaution.

Your answer

This is not as straightforward a question to answer as it might at first seem. Your answer needs to be phrased in such a way as to make it clear that you have nothing to hide and you would be quite happy to provide details of referees but that this should only be done once your application is subject to a firm job offer. This is an entirely reasonable request and deserves to be respected.

EXAMPLE

I understand the importance of references and would be delighted for you to have a word with my referees, I'm confident they'll be very supportive of my application. However, my decision to change jobs is quite a sensitive issue particularly with regard to my current employer, so I would prefer it if we could leave the issue of referees until such time as we might be discussing a firm job offer.

Chapter **4**

The top 25 tough questions: taking the heat

I made the point in the previous chapter that many questions which you might initially believe to be tough are actually just more aggressively phrased versions of classic questions. Any questions which neatly fit this definition we have covered in detail in the previous chapter.

Unfortunately, the fact remains that there are a number of questions which can only be defined as tough, mean or downright nasty.

There's absolutely no need to panic, though. As always, preparation is the key. If you're aware that you might get asked a particular question and you've taken the time to think it through beforehand and prepare an answer, then you've won more than half the battle.

One of the main reasons interviewers ask such questions is to throw candidates off balance. I remember, early in my career, one interviewer asking me bluntly, 'Can you make tea?' They also want to see how you react under stress and pressure. It is essential that you remain calm under fire and don't give the interviewer the impression that they've rattled you in any way. If you're prepared for the question then you'll be a whole lot less likely to panic.

Turning negatives into positives

An identifying feature of tough interview questions is that they will either address a negative issue or they will be phrased in such a manner as to lead you into giving what seems to be a negative response.

The key to all answers is to identify how you can turn this potentially negative situation into a positive one, which really isn't too difficult when you know how.

No beating about the bush

Another identifying feature of many tough interview questions is how direct they are. Often they lack subtlety, coming straight to the point in order to instantly put you on the spot. Rather than seeing this as a threat, you should try to see it as something positive; at least you're unlikely to misunderstand the question.

1. You must surely have more than one weakness?

Alternative and related questions

What would you say are your other weaknesses?

Tell me about another weakness.

The meaning behind the question

I mentioned in an earlier chapter that you should be prepared for the interviewer to ask the follow-up question, 'OK. That's one weakness. You must surely have more than one weakness?'

What they're doing with this question is trying to put you under pressure to see how you react. Most people attending an interview will have prepared one stock answer to the question, what are your weaknesses? that will cover talking about just one weakness. They're not expecting to have to think of a second weakness, let alone talk about it!

Your answer

This is only really a tough question if you haven't prepared for it. Your answer is easy enough and should be prepared along the same lines as you will already have prepared for the top 10 question, 'What are your weaknesses?' that we discussed in Chapter 2. However, you have a lot more leeway to cite an example that really isn't a weakness at all.

EXAMPLE

I suppose everybody has more than one weakness. If I had to think of another weakness I would say it's that I have a tendency to focus too much on detail. I can go to great lengths to get something just right and this can mean that it takes me somewhat longer to complete than someone who rushes the task. However, I very much believe that if something is worth doing then it is worth doing to the very best of your ability. Also, it's well known that cutting corners can just lead to more work in the long term; it's counterproductive. I recognise, though, that it's not always appropriate to complete every task perfectly and I have worked on my ability to know when good is good enough.

Word of warning

If you're up against a particularly difficult interviewer then it's always possible they will press you to give yet another example. As always, the secret is to be prepared.

2. What character flaws do you have?

Alternative and related questions

Do you have any personality defects?

The meaning behind the question

This is an aggressively phrased and potentially very leading question. The interviewer is trying to force you to expose a major weakness. It's not too dissimilar to their questioning you about your weaknesses, except that it's a much broader question and a much more personal question. Whilst they will obviously be interested in any personality defects you may have, their main purpose in asking you this question is to put you in a difficult situation and see how you handle it.

Your answer

It would be a mistake to respond directly to this question and start talking about something which is inherently going to be very negative. Whilst declaring that you have no weaknesses would be excessive, it is perfectly reasonable to state that you don't feel you have any character flaws. You can instead sidestep the question and talk about a minor weakness. When discussing potentially negative points, make sure you put some spin on it to turn a negative into a positive.

> **EXAMPLE**
>
> Everybody's character is different, but I don't believe I have any major character flaws. I suppose I can, on occasion, be overly demanding both of myself and members of my team. I can be very critical of my own work and I expect those under me to work to the same standards. I am nevertheless a patient individual and am prepared to give members of my staff a reasonable chance. Everyone makes mistakes; the important thing is never to make the same mistake twice.

3. How do you handle being criticised?

Alternative and related questions

How do you take criticism?

How did you react when you were last criticised?

Can you tell me about an occasion when your work was criticised?

Have you ever had an idea that has been criticised by someone else?

The meaning behind the question

Hearing you describe how you handle criticism will tell the interviewer a lot about you as a person and about what sort of person you are to work with. Everybody needs to be prepared to accept constructive criticism where it is due. The interviewer won't want to hire someone who reacts badly to criticism, someone who isn't prepared to listen to criticism or someone who takes it as a personal attack. If you have a problem with criticism then you're going to be difficult to manage and you're not going to get the job.

Your answer

Whilst it can be a good idea (even if you haven't specifically been asked to do so) to cite an example of a situation where you were criticised, you will need to choose your example very carefully, don't pick a major blunder, and make sure you phrase it in such a way as to demonstrate that you learned from the experience.

Yet again, you need to take what could potentially be a negative topic and turn it round so that it becomes a positive selling point. Don't fall into the trap of exposing a weakness. As always, make sure you come up smelling of roses.

For those of you who do have a problem with criticism, it doesn't really matter how you handle criticism; it's how you lead the interviewer to believe that you handle criticism which really counts.

EXAMPLE

If criticism is due then I generally welcome it. I'm very critical of my own work and I always appreciate constructive criticism and feedback from others, especially those who may have a different angle on ▶

matters or possibly more experience than I do. I was recently asked to work on a tender document for a new contract and, since this is not normally a part of my job, my experience in this respect was limited. I actually invited criticism from both my line manager and from a more experienced colleague. Whilst they were largely impressed with my work they certainly gave me constructive criticism on a number of different areas and this helped me to perfect the document. We won the contract and I've definitely learned a lot from the experience, which will be useful to me in the future.

4. What really makes you lose your rag?

Alternative and related questions

What causes you to lose your temper?
What really makes you angry?
Do you ever lose your cool?

The meaning behind the question

The gloves are off. This is a very direct and potentially very challenging question. The interviewer will know that they are immediately putting you under pressure with such a question. And that's very appropriate because this question is all about pressure, what causes you to feel under pressure and how you react under excessive levels of stress and pressure. Your answer could tell the interviewer a lot about you.

Your answer

This is one question where it would definitely be best not to give a specific example. The interviewer will not be impressed by hearing about the time you stubbed your cigarette out in your manager's coffee cup before telling them precisely where they could stick their job. Regardless of how volatile your character is you need to convey an impression of a calm, level-headed individual and one who remains as such even when the going gets tough. Everybody loses their rag sometimes, including the interviewer sitting opposite you, but it would be a mistake for you to disclose too much about yourself with your answer.

BLOOPER!

....

A candidate actually answered this question, 'I really lost my rag this morning trying to get the plastic wrapping off of some new CDs that arrived in the post. You know those plastic wrappers with the ring-pull-type thing like on cigarette packets?' Not a good answer, and on so many different levels!

EXAMPLE

I recognise that losing my temper is very unlikely to achieve anything; in fact, getting angry is generally very counterproductive. Whilst the behaviour of others can, of course, sometimes cause me to feel frustrated or even annoyed, I always focus on remaining calm and finding solutions to the problem at hand. I try to channel any negative feelings into my work because that's normally the best way of resolving the issue. Stress and pressure are facts of life and losing your rag won't fix anything.

5. How did you cope with the most difficult colleague you've ever had?

Alternative and related questions

Have you ever had problems getting on with a colleague?
Is there anyone you currently work with that you find really difficult to relate to?
What sort of person do you find difficult to work with?
Have you ever had to work with someone really difficult?

The meaning behind the question

The way in which you answer this question will tell the interviewer pretty much everything they need to know about your interpersonal skills.

When it comes to dealing with interpersonal conflict, there are three main ways in which you might react:

➤ Do you clash head-on with difficult people?

➤ Do you find ways to deal with them?

➤ Do you run away and hide?

The interviewer wants to ascertain which of these categories you fall into. It's a probing question that will not only tell them how you are likely to interrelate with your colleagues but will also speak volumes about your character in general.

Whilst it might seem blatantly obvious what makes someone difficult to work with, the interviewer will also be interested in your perception of what makes a colleague difficult.

Your answer

Convey to the interviewer that you firmly fall into the second category. You want to demonstrate that you are someone who, when faced with a difficult colleague (or customer for that matter), will find ways to deal with them to put your relationship on a more positive footing. It's a great opportunity to portray yourself as management material.

The interviewer won't want to hire a hothead who is just going to clash with their colleagues, nor do they want to hire someone who is going to be prone to being bullied. Most working environments contain at least one 'difficult' person; it's the school bully syndrome. It's a fact of life and you've got to show that you can cope with it and that you can, in spite of the difficulties, successfully work with such individuals.

Empathy is very important but it's vital to be assertive with it or you're not going to get very far.

EXAMPLE

Like everybody, I've certainly had to deal with difficult colleagues on occasion; colleagues who have failed to pull their weight, who have been too ready to blame others for their errors or who simply have an unpleasant and unprofessional attitude. I'm not afraid of making my opinion known and I believe that communication, especially in difficult or high-pressure situations, is essential in developing effective working relationships. Whilst some interpersonal conflict is inevitable, I don't believe in clashing head-on with a difficult colleague. It's much more productive to try to understand them, to reason with them and to find ways of working through any difficulties you may have. Communication is the key. You often find that someone with whom you initially had difficulties can, once you've reached an understanding, become a valued co-worker.

6. Are you able to make difficult decisions and tough choices?

Alternative and related questions

Have you ever had to make a really difficult decision at work?
What kind of decisions do you find difficult?
Have you ever had to make a tough and unpopular choice at work?

The meaning behind the question

You might think that there's no hidden meaning to this question, and that it's a very direct question as to your decision-making abilities. However, it all hinges on precisely how you define a difficult decision and your answer will almost inevitably reveal this. The interviewer wants to assess what your conception of a difficult decision is and how you feel about making such decisions.

Your answer

The secret is to establish your definition of a difficult decision. Some decisions are inevitably more difficult to make than others, but you don't want to lead the interviewer into believing you would have problems making a difficult decision if it was necessary. Rather than portraying indecisiveness (which will always be a negative point) you need to demonstrate you accept that it is a necessary evil to have to make certain difficult decisions.

This question is most likely to be asked of those in reasonably senior positions; as the saying goes, it's tough at the top. It's a good idea to focus on decisions which have a direct impact on the lives of your staff; undoubtedly the most difficult decisions any manager has to make. Most managers will, at one stage or another, have had to fire someone or make someone redundant or at the very least take the decision to discipline a member of staff.

For me, the most difficult decisions are those with the highest human cost; for example, the decision to make redundancies. However, I don't shy away from my responsibilities and I recognise that certain business circumstances can force such decisions, and that it would be potentially damaging not to firmly and efficiently make such decisions. In the last recession I had to make a number of redundancies as a result of the adverse economic climate. I certainly wouldn't claim it was easy but it was necessary to protect the business and the livelihoods of everyone else working for the organisation.

7. Why haven't you achieved more in your career?

Alternative and related questions

Why haven't you achieved more in your current/last job?

The meaning behind the question

This question is clearly a veiled criticism. It's a very clever question and can quickly separate out the weaker candidates from the stronger ones. This is a tough question because the main aim is to put you under attack to see how you handle it. As with a number of other tough questions, the way you answer is of more interest to the interviewer than an actual explanation as to why you haven't achieved more.

Your answer

Don't let this question rattle you. Don't let the interviewer put you on the defensive. Don't take it personally.

In most cases, you shouldn't fall into the trap of admitting that you feel you should have achieved more. Even Bill Gates will feel he should have achieved more in his career; it is human nature to feel you could have done better. You should instead spin this question round and throw it back at the interviewer as a statement of precisely what it is you have achieved in your career and why you are proud of that. You should also express optimism for the future.

If, on the other hand, you clearly could have achieved more in your career then you should attempt to cite some extenuating circumstances. This is inevitably going to be a weaker answer but it's preferable to stubbornly insisting that there aren't any weaknesses in your career path when there blatantly are. It's even more important in this case to express your optimism for the future; to emphasise that you are now 'back on track' and ready to make up for lost time.

EXAMPLE

I'm actually very pleased with my career to date. As I've progressed from organisation to organisation I've gained a great deal of practical experience and developed my abilities considerably. I have been responsible for a number of significant achievements; in my current role I successfully drove down stock from £1.5 million to £800k in just nine months whilst maintaining lead times, boosting working capital by £700k. I always strive to achieve my best and that is definitely a factor in my now looking for a new job. I feel that this vacancy would be a perfect next step for me because I know I can rise to the challenge and make a major contribution.

---

8. What don't you like about this line of work?

Alternative and related questions

What aspects of your job would you change if you could?

The meaning behind the question

This is a loaded question designed to talk you into disclosing potentially negative information about your attitude to your work. The interviewer is trying to gain further insight into how suited you are to this line of work and, in particular, how suited you are to the vacancy for which you are now applying.

Your answer

This can be a slippery question to answer but it's not really that difficult to get right if you understand the meaning behind the question and are able to avoid various pitfalls.

First of all, you're not going to get away with replying, 'Nothing at all.' Everybody has some aspects of their work that they don't like or at least like less than other parts. Even film stars must get fed up with having to be on set at 5 am in order to earn their £10 million fee.

Having established that you've got to come up with at least one aspect of your work that you're not mad about, it is essential to make sure you pick on something minor. After all, if there's something major you don't like about this line of work then why are you applying for this job? Preferably you should hit on one or two minor issues which almost every-one in your line of work is likely to also find objectionable.

The main thrust of your answer has to be that you do, of course, enjoy this line of work and that any downsides are only minor. As usual, turn an inherently negative question round so as to give a positive reply. Downplay your dislikes so that they appear trivial and irrelevant.

EXAMPLE

I love this line of work and so it's hard for me to say there are areas of it that I don't like but there are some areas I enjoy less than others. They're very minor, though. For example, whilst I appreciate the impor-tance of adhering to the requirements of all the compliance legislation, it does take up time that I would rather spend actually working with clients to find solutions to their problems. It can also be frustrating dealing with call centre staff at the banks because they rarely seem to have the knowledge or authority to resolve a situation and this is a fur-ther waste of time that could otherwise be better spent.

9. Where does your current employer think you are at the moment?

Alternative and related questions

What reason did you give to your current employer for your being absent to attend this interview?

Why does your current boss think you're not at work right now?

The meaning behind the question

Ouch! This really can be a nasty question. As well as being a deliberate attempt to panic you, the interviewer is also probing both your loyalty and your honesty. They'll be very interested to find out both how you handle the question and where, indeed, your current employer does think you are.

Your answer

If you're lucky your boss will know exactly where you are and your answer will be a piece of cake. In most cases, though, your boss will be blissfully unaware of what you are up to and you could have given any one of a number of excuses as to where you are. The single most important thing here is to not be exposed as a liar. You may have made up a little white lie for your current employer to explain your absence, which it's harmless, but it's not going to impress your interviewer. I hate to say it but it'll be time to cover one little white lie with another.

EXAMPLE

For obvious reasons, I haven't told my current employer about this interview. I consider it, for the time being, to be a personal matter and that's precisely what I told my boss; I would need to take a half-day today because I had a personal matter to attend to.

10. What are your current boss's weaknesses?

Alternative and related questions

What's the main criticism you would make of your current boss?

The meaning behind the question

This is a very thorny question and the interviewer knows it to be a very thorny question. It's unlikely they care very much about what your boss's weaknesses are, although they will be interested in seeing how you define weakness. But, as with many of the toughest questions, they're primarily interested in how you react to the question.

Your answer

It would be a mistake to say that your boss has no weaknesses; it'll ring hollow. However, it would also be a mistake to level too much criticism at your boss; you won't come across as being a very loyal employee; it has no relevance to your ability to do the job for which you are applying and it's unprofessional. You want to deflect this question and the secret is to tackle the question along much the same lines as you would respond to the question, 'What are your weaknesses?' Talk about a weakness that's not necessarily a weakness at all but make it sound convincing.

EXAMPLE

I'd be wary of criticising my boss because I don't think it's very professional. However, everyone has their weaknesses. My boss wouldn't be in the role they're in if their strengths didn't significantly outweigh their weaknesses. If I had to cite a weakness I would say it's that they tend to bite off more than they can chew. I don't know if it's necessarily a weakness to be overly ambitious as a result, they often seem excessively busy and overworked and, inevitably, certain items slip through the net. However, the end result is probably that they get a lot more accomplished than the average person.

11. What are your current employer's plans for the year ahead?

Alternative and related questions

Is your current employer planning to launch any new products/services?
Is your current employer planning to expand this year?

The meaning behind the question

There are two possible scenarios here. The interviewer could simply be attempting to assess how professional you are in terms of loyalty, discretion, honesty etc. Alternatively, they could be deliberately pumping you for commercially sensitive information. Sadly it is the case that some interviews are purely a pretext for extracting information from a competitor's employees. It may be hard to tell which of the two scenarios you are in but it doesn't really matter because the answer you need to give is the same.

Your answer

It's very simple. You should in no way be divulging your current employer's confidential plans. If there are any plans for new products, services etc. which are already clearly in the public domain, then you can of course talk about that. But you should resist all temptation to let the interviewer extract any other information from you. Whilst they might lead you to think it will be to your advantage to spill the beans, at the end of the day nobody wants to employ someone who could later pose a security risk.

EXAMPLE

I regret that any of my current employer's plans are of course confidential and commercially sensitive. I'm naturally honour bound not to divulge details. I'm sorry. I would of course be more than happy to talk about how the business has developed over the past 12 months and the role I played in that.

12. What reservations do you have about working for us?

Alternative and related questions

Can you see any disadvantages to working for us?

Have you ever heard anything negative about our organisation?

The meaning behind the question

The interviewer is laying a trap for you here. By assessing what reservations you might have about their organisation, they can gauge how much the position really appeals to you. If the interviewer can identify you as having any concerns or reservations about working for their organisation, then they're immediately going to have concerns themselves as to your commitment to wanting to work for them.

Your answer

There's only one way to answer this question: You don't have any reservations. And then go on to explain why you don't have any reservations or, more specifically, to reiterate what it is that attracts you to this organisation.

If you do have any reservations or have heard bad things about the organisation then you should certainly keep this to yourself, but you should also be asking yourself why you would want to be working for this organisation if you have such concerns.

I know some readers will feel that it is only natural to have some doubts about a potential employer and that it is reasonable to bring these up at interview, albeit in a polite and positive manner. I can see where you're coming from on this but if you do take this path then be warned that you are treading on very thin ice. I would vote very much in favour of sidestepping this question.

> **EXAMPLE**
>
> I don't have any reservations. I've done my research and considered the matter in detail and I have concluded that this is an excellent opportunity; one which I am eager to pursue. Yours is a rapidly growing and dynamic organisation and I am sure I will fit in well here.

13. You've been out of work for a while. Has it been difficult finding a job?

Alternative and related questions

Why have you been out of work for so long?
Why were you out of work for so long between these two jobs?

The meaning behind the question

If it's been a while since you last worked then there could be many different reasons. The interviewer wants to know precisely what the reason is and what, if any, bearing it has on your application.

Your answer

The most common reason for being out of work is, surprise, surprise, because you have been struggling to find work. But if you tell the interviewer this then it will immediately ring alarm bells. It may seem harsh, but if nobody else wants you then why should they?

You need to phrase yourself carefully so as to convey the impression that the reason you have been out of work is not because your services are not in demand but because you have, quite sensibly, been selective in your choice and that this particular vacancy meets all your criteria.

Make it clear that you have been proactive in your job hunt but that the right job isn't always available at the right time. You have consciously chosen not to leap into a new role simply in order to remain in employment.

You also need to be prepared for the interviewer to follow up by asking why you left your last job – assuming they haven't asked already.

Besides difficulty in finding work, other reasons for being out of the workplace include undertaking further training/education, raising a child, caring for another dependant, travel and ill health.

For further advice on how to handle these circumstances please take a look at Question 29, 'Why is there a gap in your CV?' in Chapter 3.

> Whilst it wouldn't have been difficult for me to find a job, I will admit that it hasn't been easy for me to find the right job. My career path is important to me, and given that I expect to remain in my next role for a fair few years, I have felt it sensible to take a few months to explore various opportunities and make sure I am selecting one which is right for me. I plan my career carefully and it is important to me that the next step meets with my long-term career goals. I have been very selective but this particular vacancy certainly meets all my criteria.

14. What's your sickness record like?

Alternative and related questions

How many days did you take off sick last year and why?
What would your current employer say if I asked them about your sickness record?
How's your health?

The meaning behind the question

Time is money; your time is your employer's money. No employer likes to lose money through staff being off sick. By directly questioning you on this topic the interviewer can gauge whether you are likely to be reliable in your attendance at work or whether you might pose a liability.

Your answer

It may well be tempting to give the interviewer a glowing account of your complete lack of illness. However, it is important to remember that the interviewer will most likely be seeking a reference from your last boss and this is just the kind of fact that they may well check up on.

If you have been absent from work as a result of a significant illness or a major accident, then you will have to disclose this but do not be embarrassed or defensive about it. The interviewer should appreciate that these things do happen, and as long as they are not given any reason to suspect that you were faking it, you should have nothing at all to be worried about. And if they're not understanding about this then do you really want to work for them anyway? If the incident was recent then it's obviously important to emphasise that the issue is now completely resolved and you are fully fit for work.

> **EXAMPLE**
>
> Generally, I have a very good sickness record. I'm rarely off work as a result of illness. I was unfortunate last year to catch flu and also to suffer a bout of food poisoning. These both kept me off work for a few days – but only a few days. I'm fit and healthy and I recover quickly. A year can easily go by without my taking a single day off sick.

15. What do you think of me as an interviewer?

Alternative and related questions

Do you think I'm a good interviewer?

The meaning behind the question

A strange question and, in most cases, totally irrelevant to your ability to do the job for which you are applying. The interviewer has two aims here:

➤ to throw you off balance and see how you react under pressure;

➤ to see how you handle the social challenge of having to appraise somebody's performance – somebody who is ostensibly a superior.

Your answer

Whilst it's perfectly acceptable to visually express a little surprise at the question (you're only human, after all), you definitely don't want to lose your composure. It is essential to remain calm under fire. And it's not a difficult question really. The key is to strike a balance between being excessively critical and being excessively sycophantic, whilst still communicating a meaningful observation.

Well, I would say you're doing a good job of assessing my specific ability to undertake this role as well as identifying what sort of a person I am; what my character is, how I interact on a social level, what I'd be like to work with, and with questions like this, you're doing a very good job of seeing how I react when I'm put on the spot!

16. If you were in my position, what questions would you ask?

Alternative and related questions

If you were interviewing someone for this job what would you most like to ask them?

The meaning behind the question

On the one hand, the interviewer is genuinely looking for a question (or questions) they haven't thought of and that they perhaps should have. On the other hand, in unexpectedly reversing your roles they're looking to see how well you can think on your feet.

Your answer

You're going to need to give the interviewer a possible question, if not a couple of possible questions. There's no way you can answer along the lines of, 'I think you've already asked everything that I would have asked.'

The only way in which this question might be tricky is if you're unprepared for it, which most candidates will be. Other than that, it's a gift horse because it gives you the opportunity to deliver a positive and pre-prepared answer to a question of your choice.

It's easy to interpret this question as, 'What would be the toughest question I could ask you?' and that is the last thing you should do. If you select your seven 'favourite' questions (or more precisely, your seven favourite answers) from the previous chapter, then it's unlikely that any one interviewer will ask you all seven. This should leave you with one or two up your sleeve to roll out on just this occasion.

Don't select from my top 10 because most of these will crop up in almost any interview.

And I would recommend you don't select from this chapter, with one exception. If you feel confident enough to pull it off then you could plump for, 'What makes you better than any of the other candidates I'm interviewing?' (see Question 18 below). I would generally recommend you stick to safer ground, though.

EXAMPLE

You've already asked many of the questions that I myself would be asking. I've obviously been to a few interviews in my time, and if I had to think of a question I would ask that you haven't already asked I think I would say, what have you learned and how have you developed over the last year/five years?

---

17. What would be the toughest question I could ask you?

Alternative and related questions

What's the toughest question you've ever been asked at interview?

The meaning behind the question

This is a question which puts you firmly on the spot. Obviously, once the interviewer knows what the toughest question is they're going to be expecting your answer. As well as seeing how you react to stress, they will be hoping to identify a chink in your armour. The main reason you'd feel a question to be tough is because it hits a raw nerve and exposes a weakness.

BLOOPER!

• •

Some people are definitely a little odd. One interviewee answered this one with, 'When you watch old films, do you ever wonder how many of the actors are now dead?' Spooky . . . I think they confused the word 'toughest' with 'weirdest'!

Your answer

There's no doubt about it, if you're not prepared for this question then it is probably one of the toughest you're likely to ever get hit with. However, if you're prepared then it's a completely different kettle of fish.

It should go without saying that you should definitely not really tell them what the toughest question is. This is an opportunity to get the interviewer to ask you a question of your choice; one for which you know you can deliver a positive and impressive response.

You obviously need to suggest a question which can definitely be described as tough, and, ideally, it should be a question an interviewer is unlikely to ask you. It makes sense to have three or four possibilities lined up just in case your favourite has already cropped up earlier in the interview. I'd suggest you pick out three or four of the tougher questions from the previous chapter.

EXAMPLE

I would say this question is probably one of the toughest you could ask me! Let me see . . . I suppose that, for me, a really tough question would be one which exposes a weakness, something along the lines of what's the worst mistake you've made at work?

18. What makes you better than any of the other candidates I'm interviewing?

Alternative and related questions

What would you say if I told you that you're not the best candidate I've seen so far?

I don't think you've got what we need. Why should I hire you?

If I told you that I don't think you're the candidate we're looking for, what would you say to try to change my mind?

Do you really feel you're up to this job?

The meaning behind the question

The interviewer may be indicating that you have failed to convince them so far that you are the best candidate for the job. Alternatively, they may just be asking you to pitch yourself. Either way, what they're really looking for is for you to give them at least one good reason why they should be hiring you and not someone else.

Your answer

As you can see there are many different ways in which the interviewer can ask you this question. Regardless of how precisely they phrase it, you should aim to answer the question as if they had asked, 'If I told you that I don't think you're the candidate we're looking for, what would you say to try to change my mind?'

To successfully answer this question you need to have a clear understanding of what the perfect candidate for the job would be and how best you match that description more so than the other candidates. But don't go overboard in your answer; you probably don't know anything about the other candidates.

This sort of question generally comes towards the end of an interview so if you feel that the interviewer's previous questions have failed to cover one of your major selling points then now is the time to speak up or for-ever hold your peace.

I couldn't comment on other candidates for the job but I can say that having now been working in this industry for over a decade, I have built up a very enviable network of contacts, which I think most other candidates would find hard to beat. I have developed successful relationships with key decision makers in numerous companies and this enables me to achieve a sales conversion rate much higher than average. I believe that my previous track record is clear evidence of what I would be able to achieve for you if you decide to appoint me to the role. I'm ambitious, highly driven and I relish a challenge.

19. I think you're overqualified for this job. Don't you?

Alternative and related questions

What would you say if I told you I thought you were overqualified for this job?

The meaning behind the question

In asking this question, the interviewer has most likely already concluded that you are, technically, overqualified for the job, but they're giving you a chance to comment on the matter; to explain to them why it is that you want this job when it is seemingly 'beneath' you.

Being overqualified for a position is a significant hurdle as employing such an individual can pose a major risk to the interviewer unless you can justify yourself. Are you desperate and prepared to take any job going whether you are really interested in it or not? Are you going to be disappointed with the role and move on quickly? Are you going to cause problems in the hierarchy?

Your answer

If you are overqualified for the position then you're going to need to address the issue. There are a number of reasons why you would be considering a job for which you are theoretically overqualified – not least a challenging economic climate with high unemployment and a scarcity of jobs. Regardless of what your actual reasons are, you need to deliver a very convincing explanation to the interviewer if your application is to survive this question.

If you don't feel you're overqualified then query this with the interviewer. If they can tell you why they think you're overqualified then it will help you to counter their objections. But perhaps you have simply misunderstood what the role entails and this vacancy isn't appropriate for you.

EXAMPLE

I realise that my last position was a management role and I certainly found that experience invaluable. However, I have concluded that what I really want to do is work directly with clients, finding solutions to their needs and subsequently delivering and implementing those solutions. I don't see this as taking a step down the ladder; it's purely a question of my seeking out a role to which I am best suited, which I will enjoy and to which I will, consequently, be able to give my all. I believe my previous management experience will undoubtedly be very useful in terms of my being better able to understand the bigger picture. However, I am definitely happier and more productive in a customer-facing role.

---

20. What will you do if I decide not to hire you?

Alternative and related questions

What effect would it have on you if we decided not to hire you?
How would you feel if your application for this job was unsuccessful?

The meaning behind the question

No, this doesn't necessarily mean the interviewer is going to turn you down. It's yet another stress question. The interviewer will also be interested in seeing how you handle rejection and what your other job search plans are.

Your answer

As with many seemingly negative questions, this is an opportunity for you to make a positive statement confirming your interest in the role, whilst making it clear that you're by no means desperate and that you know you will be in demand elsewhere. Don't react defensively or aggressively. Keep your cool and answer the question in a very matter-of-fact manner.

> **EXAMPLE**
>
> I would be disappointed. I'm very keen to get this job. It meets all my requirements and I firmly believe that I also meet all your require-ments. Yours is an organisation I can certainly see myself working well for. However, I do have a number of other applications in pro-gress for similar roles, and if my application for this job was not successful, I would continue to pursue other opportunities. But this particular role does remain my preferred choice and I hope I have demonstrated that I would be an ideal candidate for the job.

21. What do you think the chief executive thinks of this organisation?

Alternative and related questions

What do you think makes a good CEO?
What do you think of this organisation?
What type of organisation would you like to work for?
What challenges do you think lie ahead for the organisation?
If you were the CEO of this organisation, what would your priorities be?

The meaning behind the question

The interviewer is testing your leadership and management qualities by assessing your ability to see the 'big picture'. You may not be applying for a senior manager's role, but by being able to demonstrate a good overall understanding of how the organisation is managed, you will reveal your understanding of how the role you're applying for impacts on the organ-isation's performance as a whole. Prepare well for this question and you can be seen as future potential candidate for management positions right from the start. And if you are applying for a management role, answering this question well is obviously imperative.

The interviewer may also be trying to find out how much research you have done, for example, what you know about the organisation in terms of its reputation, its values or how it looks after its staff.

Your answer

You cannot know what the CEO thinks, but the good news is that you do not need to be a CEO to comment on what is important. It is your chance to let the recruiter know that you have done some research and you have identified some of the ingredients that are important to that organisation. Sometimes, an organisation will send you details of their ethos or values, which is a great help.

This question is also an opportunity to explain that this is the type of organisation you are looking to work for. Knowing about recent financial results, long- and short-term strategies, competition in the market place, expansion plans etc. would all be beneficial when it comes to answering this question well.

Also, make sure you show how you can be useful in realising the organisation's goals by quoting from your own CV and relevant parts of the job description with what you know and imagine the CEO's priorities are.

EXAMPLE

I can't be certain what the CEO thinks of the organisation, but I have done my research on what is important and I can make a guess as to what some of their thoughts might be. From reading your website and looking at the latest press releases, I can see that the current CEO has been with the organisation for a few years now and that the end-of-year results are showing very good growth and a solid rise in profits. Based on this, I would expect them to be positive, proud and pleased with the way things are going. I'm sure they are also excited about their plans to expand into both France and Ireland this year. There will, I am sure, be quite a number of challenges they will need to surmount, and as a software engineer with well-documented international experience, I feel confident I can develop the IT solutions needed successfully and as cost-effectively as possible.

Word of warning

Most interviewers will be proud of the organisations they work for, so although you may be tempted to criticise the CEO or the organisation for what appears to you to have been a mistake, you must refrain from airing any such views during the interview. Even if it is well known that the organisation is facing certain difficulties, try to be constructive, not negative, in your comments.

22. How long is your long term?

Alternative and related questions

Where do you see yourself in 5 years? 10 years?
Have you set any specific goals for the future?

The meaning behind the question

Easily interpreted as a 'curveball' question, this is just a question about your career plans phrased somewhat unconventionally. The slightly different turn of phrase suggests that there is a philosophical element involved here, but it's just there to throw you. What the interviewer wants is for you to consider your career path carefully and demonstrate that you understand how the industry and the position you're applying for impact on the definition of 'long term'.

The interviewer will also be looking to gauge your level of ambition; there is nothing negative about showing that you are keen to move up the career ladder.

Your answer

Now that you know this is in fact a sensible question, you can relax and start thinking. Depending on the circumstances, long term could be anything from a year to 10 years. That's for you to decide!

With this being my first position as a graduate, I am really keen on learning as much as possible from more experienced colleagues. My long-term goal is to progress into a management role in, say, five to seven years' time. From looking at your website and from what I have heard from others you offer many opportunities for development, but I fully recognise that it will take some time before I am ready to move into management.

23. What would you do if you caught a member of staff kissing the boss?

Alternative and related questions

What would you do if you saw a colleague out on the town when they were supposed to be on sick leave/saw someone taking stationery and putting into their own bag?

How would you deal with a colleague you caught stealing stationery from your workplace?

The meaning behind the question

There will be number of reasons the interviewer may ask this type of question, depending on the position the candidate is being interviewed for and the personal and professional qualities the interviewer is trying to probe. Management skills, common sense, integrity, sensitivity, staff management etc. are most certainly on the list. As many lasting relationships begin in the workplace, yet are often officially discouraged, it is a situation that can indeed be difficult to handle and which can be a challenge for everyone involved.

Your answer

The answer needs to include that you do not panic, that you are aware of your own position and limit of your authority, that you take time to consider the options and that you can make a diplomatic decision taking into account the impact this situation could have if discovered. It's a fine line that you'll have to tread; one which requires discretion and common sense.

It's also not as simple an issue as it first sounds . . . Is the member of staff a colleague and do you have the same boss? Is the boss male and the member of staff female or vice versa? Does this appear to be a consenting situation or was anyone trying to force it? Was there alcohol involved? Is the member of staff reporting to you and are you reporting to the boss? Did you see it in the workplace? At the Christmas party? Is it an established office romance that everyone knows about but you just haven't seen them together?

Most organisations will discourage workplace relationships and have written policies in place covering how to deal with it. However, there is no official legislation prohibiting it. We spend a great deal of our lives with our work colleagues and maintaining good personal relationships and perhaps having the odd crush makes working life more enjoyable.

EXAMPLE

That would be a very tricky situation to deal with and would present anyone with a difficult dilemma. In one sense, it would be none of my business, but someone might think I had a responsibility to raise the subject with the person themselves or with someone else in the organisation. What I think I would initially do is take myself away from the situation without getting involved. I would then take some time to consider the pros and cons and maybe discuss it with someone outside of work. What I would not do is discuss it with a colleague. Basically, I don't think I would raise it with the person concerned or with anyone more senior without very careful consideration of the impact this might have. There really isn't a simple answer.

24. Describe yourself in three words

Alternative and related questions

How do you think your colleagues view you?
What sort of person are you in a nutshell?
Describe your main strengths.
Tell me three qualities that you would bring to this organisation.

The meaning behind the question

This is quite a common question, particularly when interviewing for management positions; that's not to say it won't put you on the spot, though. It's a way of finding out whether the candidate has a realistic view of themselves, understands how they come across to others and it may also reveal if they've done sufficient research to know which qualities should be highlighted for this particular role.

The interviewer will try to gauge your suitability for the role in areas such as your ability to collaborate, your style of thinking, your leadership qualities, preferred working environment, how you deal with pressure etc.

Remember that the interviewer is interested only in the skills and qualities you possess that are relevant to the role.

Your answer

The employer is interested in hearing about your strengths as they relate to the job. In your preparation prior to the interview, look at the person specification and job description taking note of what behaviours and characteristics are important for the job. When you are asked this question at interview you can then draw attention to the strengths and qualities you possess that are a good match to the position you are applying for.

It is important that you carefully consider which adjectives you would choose and why. The difficulty lies in not being able to use whole sentences to describe yourself, which you will be used to doing. Instead, you have to find three single words that sum up your suitability for the role.

Your selection will depend on your personality and the role you're applying for.

➤ Outgoing, creative, innovative (marketing executive, events co-ordinator)
➤ Analytical, problem solver, collaborative (computer programmer, engineer)
➤ Knowledgeable, caring, responsible (nurse, care worker)
➤ Tenacious, friendly, focused (direct sales, call centre worker, sales management)
➤ Organised, analytical, driven (project manager)
➤ Dedicated, structured, strong (retail manager)
➤ Reliable, flexible, organised (PA, administrator)
➤ Authoritative, passionate, organised (teacher)

Word of warning

Avoid words which might technically be positive but which may come across badly when describing oneself, such as 'intelligent' (which you might want others to use when describing you but which you shouldn't use yourself), 'successful' (it's over the top; say 'accomplished' instead), 'humble' (no false modesty).

25. Would you rather know a lot about a little or a little about a lot?

Alternative and related questions

Are you a stickler for detail or do you prefer to take an overview?
What kind of manager do you prefer – someone who offers hands-on support or someone who leaves you to get on with your work?

The meaning behind the question

'The guy who knows a lot about one thing works for the guy that knows a little about everything.'

The idea here is to gauge whether you recognise yourself as an expert (a specialist) in your field or someone who has a broader level of knowledge (a generalist). For more technical, less people-facing roles you would be expected to prefer to be an expert (knowing a lot about a little). For a more customer-facing or people-management roles where conversational and social skills are important, having a broad surface knowledge of a number of things (knowing a lot about a little) may be preferred. For some roles, you may need to be a bit of both. Middle managers tend to be former experts who need to adapt to taking a broader view. And senior managers will have moved on to only seeing the bigger picture, relying on specialists for detailed briefings.

Your answer

The key to this answer is in the job description and in your own CV. Are you a generalist? Are you a specialist? Or are you somewhere in between?

EXAMPLE

For this role, I think the best candidate would be one who takes more of an overview rather than obsessing over the finer details. I think of myself as someone who can get on with anyone. My experience as an events co-ordinator has required a great deal of customer-facing work and I believe I have the strong communication skills this role needs. I am also used to working towards goals and targets as part of my work in sales; another area where you quickly have to be able to build rapport around whatever subjects the client want to talk about, so knowing a little about a lot has been very beneficial to me in the past and I anticipate it will carry on working well for me in the future.

Chapter **5**

Fifty less common questions: forewarned is forearmed

Some of these questions will, to a degree, be variations on the same theme as one or more of the questions I have already covered but others will be completely new to you, and whilst you are less likely to be asked them, it never hurts to be prepared.

Let's start off with some questions which talk about your current employment.

1. Can you tell me what you enjoy about your current job?

Alternative and related questions

What do you like about your current job?

What do you find most satisfying about your current job?

The meaning behind the question

The interviewer is seeking to identify what it is that you most enjoy about the work you currently do to help them gauge to what degree you're likely to enjoy this new position. It's another way in which they can spot any potential incompatibilities between you and this new job, or for them to reinforce their opinion that you are indeed a good match for the job.

Your answer

Your favourite part of your current job might well be receiving your salary at the end of each month but that's definitely not going to make for a good answer.

We've already had the question, 'What does your current job involve on a day-to-day basis?' and my advice was for you to focus on areas of your current job which most closely match the job for which you are now applying. My advice is similar for this question. In choosing which aspects of your job to tell them you most enjoy, you need to try to select aspects which will lead the interviewer to believe that you will also enjoy and perform well in this new job.

What are the most important tasks/duties/responsibilities that your current job has in common with this vacancy? Whatever they are, that's where you need to focus attention.

There's no harm in starting your answer with a general statement to the effect that you enjoy most aspects of your job but you then need to go on to give some specific examples, which will help to support your case for being an ideal fit for this new job.

> **EXAMPLE**
>
> That's a difficult question because there's a lot I like about my current job. I want to move on because I'm looking for a new and greater challenge not because I dislike my current job. But I'd say that I enjoy giving direct support to senior management in a way that really makes a difference. The contribution I make is vital to their ability to make key financial decisions, which ultimately influence the overall success of the business. I enjoy the challenge, I enjoy the responsibility and I enjoy the methodical and precise approach which is necessary for me to deliver the information that management rely upon.

Word of warning

Steer clear of aspects which are irrelevant to the job for which you are now applying. They won't help to support your case; they'll only risk damaging it.

2. What will you remember most about your last job?

Alternative and related questions

Can you tell me what you enjoy about your current job?
What is the best thing about your current job?

The meaning behind the question

This is another question designed to identify what you like best about your current job so as to test your motivations in wanting to move on and to better ascertain your suitability for the role for which you are applying. The transition from one job to the next can be a tricky time, and the interviewer wants to make sure there aren't any unexpected hurdles and that you're not likely to have any regrets.

Your answer

You need to focus on a positive. Telling the interviewer your predominant memory will be what a sadistic so-and-so your boss was is not going to come across well! Pick features that shows you in a positive light and elaborate on them in such a way that it comes across as a positive selling point for you. They've given you an excellent opportunity to subtly say nice things about yourself.

> **EXAMPLE**
>
> What I'll remember most is the team I work with. They're an outstanding team and I'm proud to have been a member. We've achieved an awful lot together, increasing production by over 20 per cent in the past year and, consequently, winning the Team of the Year award. There's a great sense of cohesion and whilst we all have our individual characters, we work very well together. I really enjoy the team spirit. Over time, the other team members have become increasingly dependent on me, as the most senior member of the team, and this is another reason why I feel the time is clearly right for me to step up to a team leader role.

Word of warning

Avoid mentioning anything which isn't going to be a feature of the job for which you're applying. If you do then the interviewer might wonder if you're really making the right decision in applying for this job or, worse, that if they do give you the job that there's a risk you might later regret it.

3. Is this the first time you have made an effort to move away from your current employers?

Alternative and related questions

Have you been tempted to leave your current employers before?

The meaning behind the question

This is a good question from the interviewer's point of view. It helps them to probe further into your reasons for wishing to leave your current employers. It helps them to get a better grasp on the way you manage your career. It helps them to better understand what makes you tick.

Your answer

It's superficially a closed question with an obvious 'Yes' or 'No' answer. But it's actually a lot more complicated than that. For a start, you need to decide if you want to tell the truth or not. The choice is yours. But, whether you answer 'Yes' or 'No', you should aim to support your answer with your reasoning and to justify that reasoning. If you haven't been tempted to leave before then why not? If you have then why did you decide to stay?

In Chapter 2 we covered the highly popular question, 'Why do you wish to leave your current position?' You need to bear in mind your answer to this when formulating your answer to this new question.

> **EXAMPLE**
>
> No, it's not the first time I've considered moving on. An opportunity did previously arise via my network. However, at the time I still felt sufficiently challenged in my role and still had plenty of things I wanted to achieve. So I declined the offer. Clearly, things are different now and I feel ready to embrace a new challenge.

Word of warning

If you answered that you have indeed previously been tempted to leave but you don't explain your reasons for deciding to stay, then there's every chance you'll be hit with the obvious follow-up question, 'Why did you decide to stay?' Pre-empt that question by explaining your reasoning up front.

4. How do you feel about the possibility of leaving your current job?

Alternative and related questions

Is leaving your current job really the best decision?
Are you sure you want to leave your current job?

The meaning behind the question

This is another question probing your motivations in wishing to leave your current job. The interviewer will be aiming to unearth any doubts you might have about moving on, doubts which might later transform into possible regrets. Your answer to this question will help to tell them how serious you are about changing jobs. Are you really committed to moving or are you just wasting their time?

Your answer

As per the previous question, this is another one where you will need to bear in mind your answer to the top 10 question, 'Why do you wish to leave your current position?'

It's perfectly acceptable to say that you will, in some ways, be sad to move on; you're only human. However, you need to twist this question round so as to seize an opportunity to reiterate to the interviewer why you wish to move on and why you feel this is the right decision for you. Focus on talking about wanting a greater challenge and greater opportunities, wanting to diversify, advance and develop and, if appropriate, taking a step up the career ladder.

> **EXAMPLE**
>
> I'll naturally be sad to leave behind many colleagues with whom I get on extremely well. That's an inevitable aspect of moving to a new and different job. But I'm mainly feeling very positive about my decision to want to move on. In my current role, I've learned all that I can reasonably learn within the organisation and I'm more than ready for a new and greater challenge. I'm very keen to achieve further professional development and this move will enable me to attain my goals. It's very much the right decision so I'm looking forward to the future rather than looking back to the past.

5. How would you describe your current employer?

Alternative and related questions

What do you think of your current employer?
What is your relationship like with your current employer?

The meaning behind the question

The interviewer is unlikely to be too interested in your current employer. What they're truffling for with this question is what your relationship is like with your current employer to better understand your motivations in wishing to leave them.

Your answer

We've previously covered the question, 'How would you describe your current boss?' Don't make the mistake of thinking this question is the same. They're specifically asking about your employer as a whole, not just your immediate boss. However, my guidelines for answering the question are very similar. Give a short but reasonably complimentary description, and, most importantly, portray yourself as a valued member of staff.

Avoid any overt negativity because, ultimately, it will reflect negatively on you. No disparaging comments; you don't want to open up a can of worms here. But, likewise, don't overly sing their praises because it may just ring hollow. After all, if they're that great, then why do you want to leave? A decent compromise is to drop in a mild criticism, which is simultaneously complimentary of your potential new employer.

EXAMPLE

I have no complaints. I'm happy with the way they operate and with the way they treat me and the way they treat their staff in general. They're good employers. They've taught me a lot; I've gained a lot of experience and I feel appreciated by them for the results I achieve and, generally, as a member of their team. I do feel that they're perhaps not as fast moving and progressive as they could be, which is probably my main reason for wishing to move on and join an organisation such as yours.

Word of warning

I've seen another expert suggest you could just answer, 'Very good' and leave it at that. However, I'd advise against this because (a) it makes you look uncommunicative and even worse, (b) it can make it look like you don't want to give a proper answer to the question, possibly because you have something to hide.

Having covered your current employment, now let's move on to some questions which talk about this new opportunity.

---

6. Wouldn't you be better suited to working in a larger/smaller organisation?

Alternative and related questions

Wouldn't you be better suited to working in a different type of organisation?

Wouldn't you be better suited to working for another organisation?

The meaning behind the question

Is it a polite way for them to tell you they're writing you off? Or is it yet another sneaky way for them to test how you react? Whilst the question might come across as superficially rather negative, it's often an encouraging sign. It might mean you just have one further hurdle to cope with and the job could be yours.

Your answer

This question reminds me of something an HR officer once said to a new member of staff at the end of their trial period: 'I think you'd be better off working for either a smaller or a larger organisation.' In this case, though, they're not telling you, they're asking and your answer has to be 'No'.

There are two main ways in which to answer this question. You can either ask them what leads them to ask such a question and hence pick up some useful clues, which will help you to counter any concerns they may have. But this will require you to think on your feet. The simpler approach is to have an answer pre-prepared which explains (or reiterates) why you feel their organisation is just the right one for you. You can draw on your answer to the top 10 question we covered back in Chapter 2: 'Why do you want to work for this organisation?' Your focus should be on what in particular attracts you to their organisation – and don't be afraid of singing their praises.

> **EXAMPLE**
>
> It's true to say that I have generally worked for larger companies. However, whilst larger companies have certain advantages over smaller ones, they also have certain disadvantages. Your company may not be the biggest in the sector but you clearly have a reputation as one of the most progressive. The company is evolving and developing rapidly, undoubtedly helped by the fact that you are smaller than some others. It makes you more manoeuvrable. I'd like to play a part in capitalising on that manoeuvrability to help the company become one of the biggest in the sector. I want to work for an organisation which is forward-thinking and isn't afraid to tackle new challenges, unlike some of the larger companies I have previously worked for.

Word of warning
Don't let them unnerve you. Don't be intimidated. Avoid being defensive.

7. How do you feel this vacancy differs from your current role?

Alternative and related questions

What do you think makes this position different from your last one?

The meaning behind the question

This ostensibly simple-sounding question is actually more complex in the hands of an experienced recruiter than you might at first think. They're not really interested in the differences themselves; they're interested in further probing into what it is that attracts you to this job and will mean that you not only survive but that you thrive in it.

Your answer

Whilst there may be any number of differences between your current or previous role and the role for which you are now applying, you must focus your answer on those aspects of your new job which appeal to you the most or which represent a new, interesting or unusual challenge. Aim to come up with at least two or three positive comments. And a useful little trick is to phrase your comments as if you've already been hired and are part of the team.

> **EXAMPLE**
>
> There are a number of differences. In particular, there's the challenge of the new international markets we'll be expanding into. I'm looking forward to working with clients beyond just the UK. I'll also have considerably more autonomy and responsibility for managing my own workload, which will make my day-to-day working life a whole lot more rewarding. And, of course, I'll be learning and helping to develop an entirely new database system, which is something I particularly enjoy.

Word of warning

However many differences you may come up with in your initial answer, be prepared for the interviewer to ask for more.

8. What reservations do you have about your ability to undertake this job?

Alternative and related questions

Do you have any reservations about your ability to undertake this job?
What reservations do you have about working for us?

The meaning behind the question

You might think this is a reasonably innocent-sounding question but it's actually far from it. First of all, the interviewer has phrased the question in such a way as to imply that you probably do have some reservations, and secondly, asking you about any reservations you may have is clearly prompting you to disclose any weaknesses. Basically, this question is a bit of a trap. If you do have any reservations then they'll end up having reservations too.

Your answer

In the previous chapter we covered the related question, 'What reservations do you have about working for us?' This question may be rather different but the answer has to remain the same.

You don't have any reservations.

More than that, explain to the interviewer why you don't have any reservations. As is so often the case, you need to turn the question back round on them and convert it into an opportunity to sell yourself.

EXAMPLE

I don't have any reservations about my ability to undertake the role. I trust I've demonstrated how my background and my experience have enabled me to develop the precise skills you are looking for and that I'm a perfect match for the job description you've outlined. I feel entirely ready and able for the challenge.

Word of warning

If, in reality, you do have any reservations then now is definitely not the time to be discussing them.

---

9. Can you describe your ideal working environment to me?

Alternative and related questions

Which of your previous working environments was the best?

The meaning behind the question

As with other questions which ask you to describe your 'ideal' of something work-related, the interviewer is attempting to assess how closely your ideal fits with the reality of their organisation. Unless you see through this aspect of their question, you could easily reveal reasons for them to notch up black marks on your application. They're testing your compatibility.

Your answer

How much do you know about the working environment in the organisation to which you're applying? Shallow as it may seem, this is what you need to be describing.

With a bit of luck, you'll already have been able to glean quite a bit of useful information from the interviewer during the course of your interview, which you can now feed back to them.

If, on the other hand, you're working completely in the dark then aim for a reasonably generic description, which represents a 'best guess' as to the type of working environment you'll be in.

EXAMPLE

My ideal working environment is one where there's a good sense of team spirit. A strong work ethic is obviously important but the human side is also important. I enjoy working with people who have a decent sense of humour and who, whilst they might take their work very seriously, don't necessarily take themselves overly seriously. I like people who are down to earth but who have a dynamic and progressive approach to their work. I really enjoy working as part of a highly committed and professional team.

Word of warning

Avoid saying anything along the lines of the way they've described their organisation's working environment as sounding like your idea of the ideal working environment. Don't be seen to be overtly sucking up. Subtly does it.

10. How do you feel we compare to our competitors?

Alternative and related questions

How would you rate us against our competitors?
What advantages do you feel we have over our competitors?

The meaning behind the question

No, the interviewer isn't just fishing for compliments. First of all, they'll be interested to see whether you've done your homework and not only know who their competitors are but also how they operate. Secondly – albeit not related to your job application – they'll have a natural curiosity as regards an outsider's opinion of their organisation and its competitors.

Your answer

A potentially tricky question but another opportunity to impress the interviewer with the research you've conducted, both on their organisation and on the sector in which they operate. Above all phrase your answer in such a manner that makes it clear to the interviewer that you'd much rather work for them than any of their competitors. But make it sound convincing and not just like you're buttering them up. What do you honestly feel sets this organisation apart from its competition? Why do you want to work for them and not their competition? Pick at least one positive difference between them and their competition and elaborate on it. Don't even think of discussing anything which is less than 100 per cent positive.

EXAMPLE

In conducting my market research when embarking on my job hunt, I took a close look not only at your company but also at your competitors. I'm aware that some of your competitors have a larger market share, higher turnover and higher profits, but what struck me about your company was its outstanding reputation for customer service and customer care. Some of your competitors may have a larger share of the market for the time being, but judging by the number of disgruntled customers posting their comments on the Internet, I'm convinced that I can work with you to ensure that we end up overtaking them. You've clearly focused on quality and reputation above all else, knowing that if you get this right then the profits will follow. That's a strategy I agree with wholeheartedly.

Word of warning

You can be skating on thin ice with questions such as this if you say something which you are unable to fully substantiate, should the interviewer decide to dig deeper. As always, conducting thorough research prior to your interview is absolutely vital.

11. What would you say is our unique selling point (USP)?

Alternative and related questions

What is our USP?
What makes us different from all our competitors?
What makes us stand out by comparison to our competition?
What makes our organisation unique?

The meaning behind the question

Following close on the heels of the previous question, 'How do you feel we compare to our competitors?' this is just another question designed to test what you know of their organisation and its place within its sector.

Your answer

If you haven't yet identified what the organisation's USP is or what combination of features makes them unique in their sector, then you really don't deserve the job for which you're applying. Most organisations have marketing departments which spend a considerable amount of time and money telling anyone and everyone who will listen precisely what they think their USP is; therefore, your answer to this question is simple. Tell it like it is.

But (there's always a but isn't there?) you may like to consider the possibility of telling them what you know of their publicly projected USP and comparing this to what you personally see as their USP (assuming, of course, that it's different). This is clearly an advanced strategy but if, for example, you actually work in marketing yourself, then I'd strongly recommend it. After all, the original question asked was, 'What would you say is our unique selling point?' What you say it is and what they say it is are not necessarily the same thing.

EXAMPLE

The USP you clearly communicate to customers is that the food you produce is entirely handmade and natural and totally avoids any artificial additives and preservatives common to so much of the pre-prepared and 'fast' food on the market today. I'd certainly not disagree with that, but I think a further USP and one which you could very possibly benefit from promoting is the fact that, unlike all your competitors, you have traditional ovens in all your shops and all baked products, right the way down to the bread for the sandwiches, are baked fresh every day on site.

Word of warning

It's very easy to mishear this question and to think the interviewer has asked what your USP is, not theirs. If in doubt then ask them to clarify. If they haven't already asked you what your USP is then it might later prompt them to do so. For ideas on how to tackle this question please refer back to the top 10 question in Chapter 2, 'What can you, above all the other applicants, bring to this job?'

12. What would be your analysis of the current trends in our industry/sector?

Alternative and related questions

What do you see as the most important trends in our industry/sector?

The meaning behind the question

They want to know if you've done your homework. A serious and committed candidate will be able to give a thorough and intelligent answer to this question. A poorly prepared candidate will most likely be completely floored by it. It's a good opportunity for the interviewer to filter out weaker candidates at a single stroke.

BLOOPER!

This answer defies belief: 'I think most people still wear suits, don't they? Apart from the ladies, of course.' The interviewer most definitely didn't ask about dress trends but that's what the candidate somehow heard!

Your answer

This question shouldn't pose you any problems because you are indeed a serious and committed candidate, right? In fact, it's a question you should relish because it really gives you a great chance to do some major showing off.

Your background research into this job should have given you a decent amount of insight into the environment in which it operates and how that industry or sector is currently evolving. Whilst it depends on the precise nature of the role for which you are applying, the interviewer generally won't be expecting you to be an expert. You just need to show them that you have done your homework and you do have a reasonable understanding of the issues at hand.

Remember that, in the core version of this question, they have specifically asked for your 'analysis', so they'll be expecting some personal commentary from you.

EXAMPLE

In terms of the marketplace, there's a lot more poaching and raiding than there used to be, and whilst I and many others see that as somewhat unethical, it's clearly something we're going to have to contend with, like it or not. On an operational basis, there's obviously a significant amount more outsourcing going on and this is clearly set to increase in the future as pressures increase to cut costs and to focus on core strengths. It's not necessarily a bad thing just so long as quality standards can be maintained. And, of course, the biggest trend has to be the increase in e-recruitment. This is having a dramatic impact on the sector, causing companies to have to evolve more and more rapidly in order to keep up with their competitors.

Next up, we'll cover a number of questions which attempt to understand your career path, plans and ambitions.

13. What aspects of your career path would you like to have been different?

Alternative and related questions

If you were just starting out in your career again, what would you do differently?

How do you feel about your career path to date?

The meaning behind the question

The interviewer is very simply looking for evidence of mistakes, failings and regrets because any such issues will inevitably tell them a lot about you and, in particular, a lot of very useful negative information.

Your answer

Everyone has loose threads; untidy parts of their life that they would like to remove. But if you were able to pull on one of those threads you could find it unravels the tapestry of your life. So, assuming you're happy with the current path of your career, it's pointless having any regrets about the past and even more pointless to admit such regrets to your interviewer.

Don't be tempted to bare your heart. You're sitting opposite an interviewer, not a psychotherapist. You have nothing to gain but plenty to lose from confessing to any disappointments. Conversely, just saying that there's nothing you would like to have been different will sound empty and portray you as lacking in imagination.

The secret to this question is to seize upon something which would not have led you down a different path, but which would have led to your arriving at your current position more quickly than you have otherwise done and then explaining why it simply wasn't possible.

An alternative approach is to shift the emphasis of the question by explaining that you're happy with your career path to date but recognise that it's now time to make a move and that it would be a mistake to carry on in your current job. The choice is yours, although I personally prefer the former strategy.

I'm very pleased with the path my career has taken to date. I've made a series of conscious decisions that have led me to where I am and to be sitting before you today. If there was any aspect of my career path that I would like to have been different then it would probably be to have embarked on my MBA a little earlier. That's easy to say now but, at the time, with the workload I had to manage, it simply wasn't physically possible for me to take on my MBA any earlier and attempting to do so would most likely have been detrimental both to my MBA and to my ability to perform my job.

Word of warning

Don't criticise other individuals or other organisations when talking about your career path. Avoid any negativity, full stop.

14. What are your greatest regrets about the path your career has taken?

Alternative and related questions

If you were just starting out in your career again, what would you do differently?

How do you feel about your career path to date?

The meaning behind the question

Like the previous closely related question, the interviewer is again looking for evidence of mistakes, failings and regrets. They're just doing so much more directly than in the previous question. The assumption is that you do have some regrets and they're hoping this question will uncover those. It's all very useful information to them.

Your answer

'Greatest regrets': it's highly emotive language, isn't it? But you definitely need to avoid giving a highly emotive answer.

Whilst this question is much more direct than the previous question, it's actually easier to answer in many ways. Don't answer it in terms of your greatest regrets; answer it in terms of whether or not you have any regrets, and answer it in terms of your not having any.

This is a question you have a very good chance of successfully dodging, without actually being seen to be dodging it.

EXAMPLE

I don't think I have any specific regrets about the path my career has taken, let alone any major regrets. I'm very pleased with the path my career has taken to date. I wouldn't say that my career has taken a path so much as that I've consciously steered my career down a certain path. All of the decisions I've made along the way have been for specific reasons and, ultimately, those decisions have led me to where I am today. There are, of course, certain things I could perhaps have done differently, but there's certainly nothing I actually regret in any way.

Word of warning

If the interviewer insists on your mentioning at least one regret then refer back to the answer you've prepared for the previous question; if they've already asked you that question, then just refer them back to the answer you gave, repeating it if appropriate, whilst emphasising that it really doesn't constitute a 'regret'.

---

15. What has been the greatest challenge you have faced in your career to date?

Alternative and related questions

What is the greatest challenge you have faced in your current job?
What has been your greatest achievement/accomplishment?

The meaning behind the question

Great challenges can mean great achievements but they can also mean great failures. The interviewer hasn't necessarily suggested you pick a challenge that you successfully surmounted, so a weaker candidate could easily be caught out here. Either way, it's a very useful question for an interviewer; they get to hear about an interesting success or failure on the candidate's part.

Your answer

Without a doubt, the very best way to answer this question is to turn the question into the top 10 question we covered back in Chapter 2: 'What has been your greatest achievement/accomplishment?'

Your greatest achievement or greatest accomplishment will undoubtedly have been a great challenge. If not, then what is there to be proud about?

If you've already been asked that question separately the best approach is to say you've already discussed that earlier and move on to talk about another major challenge. As with many other interview questions, it's a good idea to have a second answer up your sleeve.

If at all possible, try to limit your answer to a challenge in your recent career history. Avoid going too far back. As a general rule when answering interview questions, if you are forced to cite an example of something which could be seen as a negative, then aim for something far back in your career history. Conversely, if you're given the opportunity to cite an example of something positive, then aim to pick something recent.

EXAMPLE

The greatest challenge I've faced in my career to date has to be the key role I played in helping my company survive the recent recession. The company was undoubtedly ill prepared for the advent and impact of the recession; their financial reserves were just too weak. After a spate of redundancies, those of us who were left faced an uphill struggle to keep sales levels up and the costs down whilst maintaining our standards of customer service. I learned a great deal from the experience. Whilst we certainly did have a tough time of it, we successfully rode out the recession, and the cost-control measures, which I personally devised and implemented, ultimately resulted in a significantly healthier bottom line than we had had before the recession.

16. What do you think are your main career options for the next five years?

Alternative and related questions

Where do you see yourself in five years' time?
How long do you plan to stay/would you stay in this job if we offer it to you?
How far do you feel you might rise in our organisation?

The meaning behind the question

This question is very closely related to my top 10 question, covered in Chapter 2: 'Where do you see yourself in five years' time?' but is sufficiently different for us to cover it separately here. The interviewer is specifically asking what you see your career options as being. They want to know how long you feel you might stay in their organisation, how this new job fits into your career plan and how you envisage you will progress in their organisation.

Your answer

The answer to this question is really quite simple. In most cases, you will simply want to demonstrate that you are committed to this new job for the five years ahead (whether that's true or not) but that, naturally, you don't want to just stand still; you expect to be able to progress and move upwards in their organisation to their benefit as well as your own. To put it another way, you see them as your preferred career option for the whole five years ahead and aren't currently contemplating any other options. In reality, five years is a long time and you may well intend to consider other options before those five years are up but telling the interviewer this isn't going to support your case for them to hire you.

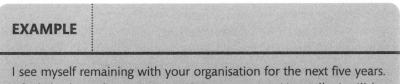

EXAMPLE

I see myself remaining with your organisation for the next five years. I feel that's my best career option at present. Naturally, I will be hoping to progress significantly over the course of those five years

▶

and having proved myself, would expect to be entrusted with greater responsibility and a higher level of autonomy. I can see that there are plenty of opportunities for promotion and for ongoing professional development within your organisation and I am keen to take advantage of them and to become a greater asset to your organisation.

Word of warning

In most cases, you should avoid being too specific and stating, for example, a particular job role you hope to be able to get in, say, three years' time. You are being recruited for a specific job and that must remain your current focus.

17. What exactly does the word 'success' mean to you?

Alternative and related questions

How do you define success?
What exactly does the word 'failure' mean to you?

The meaning behind the question

This is an interesting question designed to identify how, in the workplace, you define success, but also to give the interviewer some greater insight into your psychology and the way you think and feel about success and what your value system is.

Your answer

Everyone knows what the word 'success' means. This question, however, is asking what the word means to you in particular. So what does it mean to you? Everyone defines success slightly differently. For some it may be a job well done. For others, it may be reward and recognition for their efforts. What is it for you?

There are no right or wrong answers to this question but be sure to keep your definition restricted to the workplace, unless of course your interviewer has specifically asked you for a broader definition, not just related to the workplace.

For me, success has a number of different elements. On the one hand, it is having achieved a specific goal or goals; the satisfaction of a job well done, having achieved one's purpose. On the other hand, it's the recognition of that achievement by others. Ultimately, success is a significant motivator for me; the desire to achieve success in all that I undertake and to contribute to the best of my ability.

Word of warning

Be prepared for the interviewer to follow up this question by asking you for an example of when you've personally achieved success.

The next couple of questions address problems in your career history.

18. Why did you stay with this organisation for such a short time?

Alternative and related questions

Why did you leave that job?
Have you ever been made redundant and, if so, why?
Have you ever been fired?

The meaning behind the question

This question is related to a question we've already previously covered, 'Why did you leave that job?' The difference here is that they're curious as to not only why you left that job, but also why you left it after 'such a short time', the definition of a 'short time' varying, of course. The interviewer is hunting again for possible skeletons in your cupboard.

Your answer

If you only stayed in a job for a short time then there was obviously a reason for this, but it may not necessarily be a positive selling point for you. Employers are always wary of hiring people who might not stay for long and especially people who have done a fair bit of 'job-hopping' in the past.

If the answer to the question is that you were either made redundant or fired, then please refer back to Question 27 in Chapter 3, where I cover how to handle these specific cases.

However, if you left of your own volition then why? Problems with your boss? Problems with a colleague? To deal with these, I'd suggest you refer back to the advice given under the top 10 question in Chapter 2: 'Why do you wish to leave your current position?'

But there are, of course, many other possible reasons; for example,

➤ you found the job you took didn't turn out to be as advertised;

➤ you found the job you took changed dramatically, for example, due to restructuring;

➤ the next job you took was an opportunity not to be missed.

My advice is very simple. Just tell it like it is. You made a positive move for positive reasons with the intention of achieving a positive outcome simple as that.

EXAMPLE

Shortly after I started with the company, external management consultants were called in and tasked with undertaking a major restructuring. Whilst my role wasn't made redundant as such, it did change out of all recognition and it simply wasn't the job I signed up for. In particular, the marketing element was completely removed from my job description and yet that is my main interest and was what I had hoped I would be focusing on when I initially agreed to take the job. I, therefore, felt I had to look for a new job, one which would enable me to continue on my desired career path and that led to my successfully being hired for my next job.

Word of warning
As always, don't let this question tempt you into saying anything negative or critical of any previous employers you have had.

19. Why did you stay with this organisation for such a long time?

Alternative and related questions

Why didn't you move on sooner from this organisation?

The meaning behind the question

There are both good and bad reasons for staying with any one employer for a long time. The interviewer is checking whether they might be able to unearth some of the bad reasons. Their main concern will most likely be that you might have become set in your ways as a result of staying too long with one organisation and will struggle to cope with and adapt to new challenges.

Your answer

In your answer what you must aim to achieve is to portray the fact that you stayed with that organisation for 'such a long time' as a positive thing, as a conscious decision you made. You definitely don't want to give the impression that you lack initiative and just drifted. Maybe you did just stay there because you were happy and secure and quite content with the status quo, but that's not the kind of answer which is going to impress the interviewer.

If you undertook more than one role within that organisation, for example, you gained promotion and moved up in the organisation, then that's all you really need to say. However, shouldn't your CV make that quite clear already?

Maybe you did only undertake the one same role for all your time in the organisation but, whilst your job title may have stayed the same, can you perhaps tell them how your job description evolved over time with new and interesting tasks and challenges?

If your work is largely project based then you could convey how, with your handling one different project after another, it felt more like a series of different jobs rather than just the same job, because it was always changing.

Above all, shift the focus onto what you learned and how you developed during your time with that organisation, in particular useful, transferable skills.

I chose to stay within that organisation because my work always remained an interesting challenge. Over the course of the decade, the company grew from a small outfit with just five employees to a much larger organisation with well over 50 employees. It changed so significantly that it didn't actually feel like I was necessarily working for the same organisation. Clearly, the way an organisation with just five employees operates is very different to the way in which one with over 50 employees operates. Whilst my actual job title may not have changed over the years, the actual nature of my work evolved and changed rapidly. The job I was doing when I left the company bore very little resemblance to the job I first took when the company was just starting up. With each new year, I learned new and valuable skills and from having been there from the beginning, I am fortunate enough to have gained very useful experience in every department, from finance through to marketing, including extensive experience which is directly relevant to the job for which I am now applying.

Now for a few questions about coping with stress and pressure.

20. Are you able to multitask?

Alternative and related questions

How good are you at multitasking?
Can you give me an example of how you multitask?

The meaning behind the question

Multitasking is a popular business buzzword. Whilst I personally think this is rather a silly question, that's not to say that it's not a popular one. No hidden meaning, except perhaps that the interviewer might want to make sure that you actually understand what multitasking is.

Your answer

As it happens, most people don't really understand what multitasking is.

Many busy people will claim to 'multitask' so as to help them get done all that needs to be done. However, research has shown that people just appear to be handling more than one task at the same time and that multitasking is largely counterproductive, the lack of attention given to any one particular task resulting in (a) that task taking longer than it would otherwise have done and (b) that task being more prone to errors, which then consume more time (albeit perhaps later on) to be corrected. Greater efficiency is actually achieved by being able to concentrate fully on one task at a time.

There are times when we have no choice but to multitask. You're busy writing up a report when an important and urgent email pops up on your computer, and simultaneously, a colleague steps up to your desk to have a quick word about something. But don't delude yourself into thinking that being able to multitask all the time is in any way desirable as a form of time management. In the above scenario, you may be able to cope with the three different tasks demanding your attention but not very effectively.

In answering this question, make it clear to the interviewer that you are aware of this distinction, but at the same time, point out that you are capable of multitasking if necessary.

EXAMPLE

It does depend how you define multitasking. I've read that, when multitasking, people just appear to be handling more than one task at the same time and that it's largely counterproductive. Sometimes, of course, I have no choice but to multitask, dealing with several different issues simultaneously; for example, finishing off an urgent email whilst taking an important phone call. Whilst it's obviously not an ideal way to work, I'm certainly more than capable of multitasking in this fashion when necessary. It's a matter of concentration.

---

21. Can you juggle a number of different projects simultaneously?

Alternative and related questions

How many projects can you handle at one time?

The meaning behind the question

If the interviewer is asking this question, you can be reasonably sure that handling multiple projects at the same time is going to be a feature of your new job. The interviewer wants to see if you are going to be able to cope with this and how. They'll be looking for sound evidence of your abilities in this respect.

Your answer

You might think this question is very similar to the previous one but it's not. Simultaneously juggling numerous different projects is definitely not the same as multitasking.

There's only one correct answer to this question and it's a resounding 'Yes'. Go on to back up your 'Yes' with some evidence, preferably an example. The interviewer is unlikely to be asking you this question unless you have previous experience of project management, so you should be able to draw on a decent example from your career history. An unqualified 'Yes' is a worthless answer. It has to be supported by some proof.

EXAMPLE

Yes. I've had plenty of experience handling a very full workload and dealing with numerous different projects simultaneously. When starting out in my current job, I came in to a situation where they were behind schedule on a number of projects and yet also had several new projects which needed to be started. I certainly had my hands very full indeed; it was quite a juggling act. I persuaded the management to allocate sufficient resources so we could complete the overdue projects without suffering further financial penalties and I simultaneously got us going on the new range of projects as quickly as possible so as to not disappoint the clients. It was very hard going but I soon got things under control, and once the backlog had been cleared and we were up to date, we were able to consistently adhere to timescales and deadlines in the future.

22. How do you handle rejection/ disappointment/failure?

Alternative and related questions

Can you tell me about a time when you have failed to achieve a goal?

How do you handle being criticised?

The meaning behind the question

There are really three different questions here but they're all very closely related. The interviewer is trying to assess how you deal with adversity, whether that adversity is in the form of rejection, failure or some other disappointment. It's also a question which gives them a useful opportunity to potentially pinpoint a particular occasion when you experienced such adversity.

Naturally, assessing how someone handles adversity says a lot about them as a person. The interviewer won't want to hire someone who can't handle it when the going gets tough.

Your answer

When the going gets tough, the tough get going!

Rejection, disappointment, failure, everyone experiences these from time to time during the course of their careers, even renowned business superstars like Sir Richard Branson. But one trait which sets people like Sir Richard Branson apart from some others is that when they do get knocked down, they always get back up again. Not only that but when they get back up, they become stronger, having learned as much from the experience as they can.

This is what you need to aim to communicate to the interviewer in your answer. Try to avoid giving a specific example unless they force you to. Just concentrate on speaking in general terms about how you handle adversity. Take what could potentially be a negative topic and turn it round so that it becomes a positive selling point. Show them how you can benefit from adversity.

I'm certainly realistic enough to appreciate that things don't always go the way one would hope or expect them to go and that the occasional disappointment is a fact of life. But I feel that what's most important is how one handles such circumstances. I endeavour to learn as much as I can from any possible failures; they really are excellent learning opportunities and they can be a blessing in disguise in that sense. And it's always important to focus on the future rather than dwell on the past. If at first you don't succeed, try, try again.

Word of warning

Even if you don't give the interviewer a specific example, you will have to be prepared for the possibility that they will push to get one out of you. If you do have to cite a real-life event then try to pick something which isn't too negative, try to pick something which is reasonably far back in your past, and, most importantly, try to pick something where the blame, if any, wasn't solely attributable to you and you alone. For example, your company having failed to win a valuable contract would work well as an answer. If possible, you can go on to outline what was learned from the experience and how this knowledge was put to good use in the future.

The next few questions deal with your perception of teamwork.

23. How do you deal with interpersonal conflict?

Alternative and related questions

How did you cope with the most difficult colleague you've ever had?
Have you ever had problems getting on with anyone?

The meaning behind the question

The interviewer is seeking to get a handle on how you are likely to react when faced with interpersonal conflict, in particular whether you know the right way to react and what your relationship-building skills are like.

This question is similar in nature to the tough question I covered back in Chapter 4: 'How did you cope with the most difficult colleague you've ever had?' The key difference is that this question asks how you cope with difficult people and difficult interpersonal situations in general, whether with a colleague or with anyone else.

You want to show the interviewer that you won't clash head-on with people, or run away and hide. You'll simply take the professional option of finding ways to deal with them, to put your relationship on a more positive footing.

And I'd suggest you start your answer off on the right foot by pointing out that you generally manage to avoid conflict most of the time.

EXAMPLE

I'm not the kind of person to get drawn into interpersonal conflict, but sometimes it's unavoidable. In such cases, I'm not afraid of making my opinion politely but firmly known and I believe that communication is essential, especially in situations involving conflicting points of view. I certainly don't believe in reacting aggressively, nor do I believe in ducking out of any confrontation. It's much more productive to try to understand people, to reason with them and to find common ground and ways of working through any difficulties there may be. Communication is key, so is seizing the initiative to tackle the problem.

Word of warning

Be prepared for the interviewer to follow up this question by asking what you would do if, despite your best efforts, you remained in conflict with someone.

---

24. What do tact and diplomacy mean to you?

Alternative and related questions

Can you describe a situation where you've been tactful?
Can you describe a situation where you're been diplomatic?

The meaning behind the question

No hidden meanings here. Tact and diplomacy are invaluable life skills and the interviewer wants to assess your capacities in this respect.

Your answer

What is tact? Well, it's about your skill in dealing with others, particularly difficult people and in difficult situations. And diplomacy? Well, it's very similar really! Tact and diplomacy are inextricably linked. It's all about how well you deal with other people and it follows hot on the heels of the previous question.

Whilst it's frequently important to be assertive, at other times you have to know when to bite your tongue. Empathy is vital for effective relationships. There's a time and a place to assert yourself and a time and a place to be a little more mindful of what you say. Show the interviewer that you understand this important distinction.

EXAMPLE

Tact and diplomacy are all about skill and sensitivity in dealing with others, particularly when dealing with difficult people and tricky situations. I'm certainly capable of asserting myself when necessary, but I'm equally capable of carefully controlling what I say if there's a risk of hurting someone else's feelings or causing some other negative and counterproductive reaction. It's a fine line one has to tread and it requires a great deal of empathy. Understanding other people and empathising with the way they think and feel are essential to effective relationships. It's also a question of context. You may find that you can say something to someone in private which it would be a very bad idea to say in the presence of others.

Word of warning

If you're asked to describe a specific situation then you must choose one which portrays you in a positive light without being undiplomatically critical of former bosses, colleagues and others. It's a good idea to pick a situation involving a difficult client or customer, although, again, try to be tactful when describing them.

25. What makes for a successful team?

Alternative and related questions

What would be your ideal team?

The meaning behind the question

Your perception of what makes for a successful team will be a factor of what you see as being a successful working manner and also how you perceive your ideal team to be. Your answer will give the interviewer a lot of useful information as to both your capabilities and your compatibility. It'll give them insight into what kind of a team player you are.

Your answer

This isn't the easiest of questions to answer. But given that you can prepare a neat little answer well in advance, it shouldn't be one of the most difficult either.

Teamwork is essential in the vast majority of working environments. It requires four core abilities:

> ➤ The ability to communicate effectively with others.
> ➤ The ability to recognise and understand the viewpoints of others.
> ➤ The ability to appreciate the contribution you are expected to make.
> ➤ The ability to build strong interpersonal relationships.

A successful team player will possess all of these qualities and a successful team is clearly comprised of successful team players.

Show the interviewer that you understand these key teamwork factors.

EXAMPLE

For me, what really makes for a successful team is clearly the people within that team. Communication is obviously key. Teamwork requires you to communicate effectively with others, recognising and understanding their viewpoints and appreciating the contribution you are expected to make. Communication is essential to good working relationships where each individual is working towards the ▶

achievement of shared aims and objectives. Trust is also a key factor in ensuring the success of working relationships, as is respect. If the team members trust and respect each other then they'll inevitably work well together towards their common goals.

Now, half a dozen questions on management and leadership.

26. Would you describe yourself as a good manager?

Alternative and related questions

Are you a good manager?
How would you describe yourself as a manager?

The meaning behind the question

The interviewer is specifically looking for you to provide them with an explanation as to why you think you're a good manager. If you're up for a management role (which you most likely are if they're asking you such a question), then your answer could be very revealing for them.

Your answer

Well, you're not exactly going to describe yourself as a bad manager, are you? Of course you're a good manager and you're going to tell the interviewer precisely why that is the case.

So what makes for a good manager?

➤ Good managers develop good working relationships with their subordinates.

➤ Good managers align the aims of their employees with those of their organisation.

➤ Good managers set challenging but realistic targets.

➤ Good managers use motivational techniques to facilitate the achievement of goals.

➤ Good managers are fair and treat their subordinates equally and objectively.

➤ Good managers demonstrate empathy, making people feel that their opinions are recognised.

➤ Good managers demand the best of people but are aware of their limitations.

➤ Good managers are prepared to take appropriate measures with those who fail to perform.

➤ Good managers praise in public but criticise in private.

➤ Good managers delegate tasks to others who can best handle them.

➤ Good managers inspire their subordinates.

I could go on but it's already a long list.

In answering this question, aim to pick up on several of these qualities; you won't want to repeat the whole list; just pick a few you feel are particularly strong points for you and which you feel are of particular relevance to the post for which you are applying.

EXAMPLE

Yes, I would. I believe I'm particularly good at motivating my subordinates. For example, I aim to align their aims with those of the organisation. Once an employee is able to understand and empathise with the overall aims of the organisation, they are normally much more motivated to help achieve them. I also believe I'm good at getting the best out of people whilst being aware of their limitations. I strive to set challenging but realistic targets and ensure people are treated fairly, equally and objectively.

Word of warning

A natural follow-up to this question will be for the interviewer to ask you to cite specific examples of where you demonstrated the qualities you've mentioned. Be ready with appropriate answers.

27. Do you really think you're management material?

Alternative and related questions

Are you sure you have management potential?

The meaning behind the question

The interviewer is likely to ask this question if the job you're applying for would represent your first step up into a management role, or if you've only just recently moved into management in your current or last role. They're not by any means suggesting that you're not management material; they're just asking for you to prove to them that you are.

Your answer

In formulating your answer you need to draw on some of the ideas we covered in the previous question. Your answer to the question obviously starts with a 'Yes' but then needs to go on to give the interviewer some evidence to back up your assertions and to show confidence in your decision to move into management.

Look back to the last question to see what makes for a good manager and mention a couple of those qualities, supporting your answer with a statement as to why you now feel ready for a management role.

> **EXAMPLE**
>
> Yes, I do. In my current role, I'm the most senior and experienced member of the team, and in all but my job title, I'm already undertaking many elements of a management role. The team is highly dependent on me and most of my time is taken up in supporting and managing the team members so that they are better able to undertake their own roles. I have extremely good working relationships with my team members and seek to extract the best from them whilst being aware of their individual limitations. I'm also responsible for training and coaching new team members. Consequently, I feel that now is definitely the right time for me to take a step up to a management-level position, hence my applying for this role within your organisation.

28. What is your attitude to delegation?

Alternative and related questions

Do you delegate?
Do you know how to delegate?
Do you have difficulties with delegation?

The meaning behind the question

Delegation is one of the most important management skills. The interviewer wants to know if you understand the importance of delegation and whether or not it's something you're capable of doing effectively.

Your answer

If you have people to whom you can reliably delegate a task and within whose job function it is to carry out such a task, then you should delegate it. So much time is lost by handling tasks which would be best delegated to someone else. It's a manager's job to delegate and to supervise that delegation; it's not possible or desirable to do everything yourself single-handedly.

The perfectionists amongst us often have considerable difficulty with delegation. Perfectionists tend to fear that a task, once delegated, simply won't be carried out to their own high standards. This may be true but does it actually matter? Whilst perfection is always highly desirable, it's often not very practical.

Show the interviewer you appreciate that delegation is a necessity and that you know precisely how to go about delegating tasks.

> **EXAMPLE**
>
> I believe that delegation is an essential management skill. It's a manager's job to delegate and to supervise that delegation; it's not possible or desirable to do everything yourself single-handedly. Of course, it's often a judgement call. You can find yourself spending more time explaining how to carry out a task than it would have taken you to complete it yourself. You have to weigh up how long it will take to explain to someone else how to undertake the task by comparison to how long it would take to just do it yourself. Small one-off tasks are typically best done yourself but lengthier tasks, or tasks which are likely to need to be repeated in the future are often best delegated.

29. Can you give me an example of a time when you had to lead from the front?

Alternative and related questions

Can you give me an example of a time when you have displayed leadership qualities?

The meaning behind the question

The interviewer knows it's very easy for you to say that you're capable of leading from the front. What they want with this question is for you to prove that to them.

Your answer

The interviewer has used the word 'lead' here. Leadership and management may be related but they're not the same thing. Leaders demonstrate vision. Leaders inspire others with that vision. Leaders are capable of thinking outside the box.

If you're being asked this question then you're most likely up for a reasonably senior management position and so should be more than capable of coming up with an appropriate example.

EXAMPLE

I frequently have to lead from the front. To give you a recent example, in my current role I initiated the design and implementation of a completely new database system. The plan was met with considerable resistance from the day-to-day users of the old database system who were happy with the status quo and didn't see the need for change. Whilst it's true that the old system did an entirely satisfactory job, I had identified a variety of weaknesses and inefficiencies and was convinced we could create a new system, which would be at least 25 per cent more efficient, resulting in considerable savings. I discussed my proposed changes with existing users and managed to bring them round to my way of thinking, emphasising that any disruption would only be short term and that the long-term gains would more than justify the project. Ultimately, not only did I manage to persuade them to follow my vision but I also got them greatly involved in the process, providing a lot of valuable and relevant ideas and feedback.

30. Have you ever had to fire or lay off a member of your staff?

Alternative and related questions

Are you able to make difficult decisions and tough choices?

The meaning behind the question

This question is clearly related to the question we covered in the previous chapter: 'Are you able to make difficult decisions and tough choices?' The interviewer wants to establish if you've ever had to make a difficult decision of this nature, and if so, how you handled it and how you felt about it, or if not, how you would feel about it. The chances are that the role for which you're applying may require you to handle such situations in the future.

Your answer

If you have had to perform this inevitably unpleasant task then a simple 'Yes' definitely won't suffice. The interviewer will want you to describe the situation in detail and how you handled it. I'd suggest you refer back to the example I gave in the previous chapter under Question 6. That should help to give you some ideas to formulate your answer.

If, on the other hand, you've never had to fire or lay off a member of staff then your answer could, of course, just be a simple 'No'. But I'd suggest you follow that up by demonstrating that you would be capable of doing so if it were necessary.

No. But, although I've never had to do this in the past, I'm not one to shy away from my responsibilities and I fully recognise that such decisions do need to be made from time to time. It's not a task I'd take lightly, of course. But, if it came to it, I'd be quite capable of handling the situation and ensuring I complied with the necessary procedures and legislation.

31. How would you describe your ideal team member?

Alternative and related questions

How would you describe your ideal subordinate?
What would be your ideal team?

The meaning behind the question

In describing their ideal team member, most candidates will automatically and subconsciously describe how they see themselves as a team member. That makes this a very interesting question for a trained interviewer. It's another question which will give them insight into what kind of a team player you are.

Your answer

This is really quite an easy question to answer. Focus on two or three positive qualities in a team member, aiming for ones which are universally popular.

EXAMPLE

My ideal team member is someone who is firmly committed to the common goals of the team, someone who is not afraid to roll up their sleeves and 'muck in' to get the job done, someone who is prepared to take personal responsibility for getting the job done. Loyalty is obviously also important, loyalty to their colleagues, their management and to the organisation as a whole. They also need to be a good communicator because communication is the key to successful working relationships.

The next couple of questions discuss personal and professional development.

32. In what ways do you intend to improve upon your performance?

Alternative and related questions

How do you think you can improve upon your performance?
Do you think you need to improve upon your performance?
Can you tell me about your last appraisal?
What areas for improvement were identified at your last appraisal?
What training needs do you have?

The meaning behind the question

This is an interesting question, specifically because, by implication, it is suggesting that there are indeed ways in which you need to improve. It's a question an interviewer might well ask as an immediate follow-up to the question we covered previously in Chapter 3, 'Can you tell me about your last appraisal?' This question is designed to prompt you to admit precisely where there is room for improvement in your performance. In some ways it can be seen as a version of the top 10 question, 'What are your weaknesses?'

BLOOPER!

Quite astonishingly, one candidate replied to this question, 'Well, if I'm happier in my new job, I obviously won't be chucking as many sickies as before.' I kid you not!

Your answer

Are they asking in what ways or in what areas? And does it really make any difference?

You're kind of damned if you do and damned if you don't with this question! It's a Catch-22. If you say you feel there aren't any ways in which you need to improve upon your performance, then you'll come across as arrogant and as someone who is unlikely to develop further because they don't even perceive the need for further development. Conversely, if you do talk about specific ways in which you intend to improve upon your performance, then you're immediately admitting a weakness.

The best solution is to keep your answer pretty general, and without declaring any specific area of weakness, emphasise that you are always looking for ways in which you can improve upon your performance and that you're always open to training and development opportunities. Alternatively, you can mention a specific area provided that it is an area which is not critical to your ability to undertake the role for which you are applying.

EXAMPLE

I'm always looking for ways in which I can improve upon my performance; I'm always open to training and development opportunities. Everyone always has room for improvement; you can never be too good at anything. For example, I find I am now required to give presentations from time to time and, whilst I'm generally happy with the way I handle these, it's fair to say that I've not had any prior training in this, so I am just about to embark on an evening course to help me to improve upon this aspect of my work.

Word of warning

Admit to any specific weaknesses and you could immediately eliminate yourself from the running. However, if you don't mention any specific areas for improvement, there's always the chance that the interviewer may go on to press you to discuss one. In this case, your answer should be along the lines of my example above.

33. How has your current job prepared you for greater challenges/responsibility?

Alternative and related questions

In what ways has your current job prepared you to take on greater challenges/responsibility?

How do your skills and experience match the job description/person specification?

What have you learned in your last job?

The meaning behind the question

The interviewer is driving at what you have learned and how you have developed in your current (or last) job, which could now be of use to you and to them in the job for which you are applying, with specific regard to your ability to take on new challenges and responsibilities.

Your answer

Why are you looking to move on to a new job? The chances are that greater challenges and greater responsibility are pretty high on your list of reasons. You need to demonstrate to the interviewer that you're ready for this and explain why.

The key to this question is to cite specific examples, which are pertinent to the job you're now applying for.

You should have a very clear idea of the key requirements of this vacancy. Use those as your guide when picking your examples, aiming for two or three examples which you can turn into strong selling points.

EXAMPLE

My current job has prepared me in many ways to take on new and greater challenges and responsibility. This is one of my main reasons for wishing to move on to a new job; to capitalise on what I have learned. As I became increasingly proficient in my role, I was entrusted with training and coaching newer members of staff, something I enjoyed and found very rewarding. I was also asked to participate in increasing numbers of management-level meetings to

▶

represent matters from the point of view of the 'shop floor'. Also, I was called upon to deputise for our manager and oversee operations whenever he was away. I consequently feel I've reached the level where I'm no longer sufficiently challenged by my current role and am keen to learn and develop further; it's clearly the right time for me to move onwards and upwards into a management role.

Now for a few questions about your interests outside work.

34. What book are you reading at the moment?

Alternative and related questions

What was the last film you saw?
What's your favourite book?

The meaning behind the question

This is obviously quite a personal question and the interviewer will be aiming to learn a number of different things from the question. For a start, they'll be interested to see if you do in fact read. More than that, they'll be interested in seeing what you read and what you have to say about it. It's not quite a psychological question but it's not far from it. What you read will inevitably tell them a bit about your personality.

Your answer

It's generally important to be seen to be a reader. You may love reading. You may hate it. Either way, you need to have an example ready and not just a made-up one. You will actually need to read a book in order to be able to effectively answer this question.

Beyond that, there is no right answer to this question. You obviously need to choose your example reasonably carefully. If you're applying to work for a French company then telling them you're currently reading *1000 Years of Annoying the French* by Stephen Clarke is probably going to come across badly. Likewise, it's hard to see any circumstances in which they'll be impressed by your reading Barbara Cartland . . . But that doesn't mean you have to tell them that you are currently ploughing through Tolstoy's *War and Peace* nor that you spend your bedtimes engaged with the latest cutting-edge management tomes. I'm just asking that you choose carefully.

Don't just tell the interviewer the title of the book. Go on to tell them a bit about it – at the very least just to prove that you're not making it up. In any case, if you don't tell them a bit about it then they'll be sure to ask. You should also be prepared for the possibility that they may have read the same book themselves, in which case you can definitely expect a longer chat about it.

EXAMPLE

I'm currently reading *Disturbing the Peace* by Richard Yates. I saw the film *Revolutionary Road* and went on to read the book and I enjoyed it so much that I'm now moving on to work my way through Richard Yates' other titles. *Disturbing the Peace* is not one of his best-known works but I find its semi-autobiographical nature particularly fascinating. You can tell that he has first-hand knowledge of what he's writing about. It's not exactly a happy book, by any means. But it's very compelling and gives a lot of insight into Richard Yates and the troubled life he led.

Word of warning

The interviewer may specifically ask for either a fiction or a non-fiction book, so it's best to have examples ready for both cases.

---

35. What newspaper do you take?

Alternative and related questions

What newspaper do you take and why?
Do you know what the current news headline is?

The meaning behind the question

This question is closely linked to the next question we'll be covering, 'Are you interested in current affairs?' and could be asked either before or after that question. In asking what newspaper you take, the interviewer will certainly be aiming to establish if you are interested in current affairs but they'll also be discreetly probing your values.

Your answer

This can be a surprisingly difficult question to answer. Common wisdom has it that the newspaper someone reads says a lot about their political, intellectual and even class values. What images spring to your mind when you think of readers of the following newspapers: *The Guardian, The Sun, The Independent, The Daily Telegraph*? They each conjure up a very different kind of person don't they? The question you have to ask yourself is what kind of a person you need to be.

You're certainly within your rights to simply tell the truth and you're also within your rights to tell the interviewer what you think they might want to hear (although guessing what that is can often be tricky). In all cases, though, you'll need to be prepared for them to ask you why you choose that particular paper. But I'd suggest avoiding the tabloids; it makes for an easier answer.

By the way, just in case you were wondering, telling the interviewer that you don't read any newspapers isn't going to reflect well on you. Conversely, reading more than one newspaper is, of course, perfectly acceptable.

EXAMPLE

I read *The Independent*. I recognise that all newspapers, *The Independent* included, inevitably have various editorial biases but I feel *The Independent* gives a particularly well-balanced view of the world and what's happening in the world without having too much political bias. I also check the BBC News website each day. Between them, I believe I'm getting a reasonably well-rounded insight into current affairs.

Word of warning

The obvious follow-up to this question is for the interviewer to ask about an issue, or, if you're unlucky, a specific article that has recently taken your interest. Just make sure you're ready for that.

36. Are you interested in current affairs?

Alternative and related questions

Do you know what the current news headline is?
Which news story has recently grabbed your attention?
What would you do to improve the state of the country's finances?

The meaning behind the question

This isn't exactly a trick question. It's just that they're not just asking if you're interested in current affairs; they're asking you to prove you're interested in current affairs and you need to be prepared and ready for that.

BLOOPER!

A friend of mine was recently stunned by one interviewee's answer to this question: 'Oh, yeah, I can't believe who Jordan's dating now!'

Your answer

For a start, your answer to the question has to be 'Yes' if you are to successfully convey to the interviewer that you are a well-informed and well-rounded individual. You should then go on to pre-empt the obvious follow-up question in which the interviewer will ask for a specific example of something which has taken your interest in the news recently. Not only that but you need to be prepared for the interviewer to want your opinion on the matter – so as to test your analytical skills. Just don't say anything controversial or likely to shock.

EXAMPLE

Yes, I read *The Independent*, I keep an eye on the BBC News website and I normally listen to the news in the car on the way home. I watch very little television, but between my newspaper, the Internet and the

radio, I really don't need to in order to keep abreast of what's going on in the world. Like many people, I've been particularly interested recently by the ongoing developments in the Arab world. It's going to be fascinating to see how that continues to unfold.

A number of interviewers fancy themselves as amateur psychiatrists, so coming up next are four questions such interviewers may ask you.

37. If you won the lottery what would you do?

Alternative and related questions

If you won the lottery would you stop working?

The meaning behind the question

This question isn't just one of silly speculation. What it'll tell the interviewer is what your priorities are outside your work and just how much of a priority your work is. That can be very revealing indeed.

Your answer

I once saw a cartoon which asked the alternative question, 'If you won the lottery, would you stop working?' and the reply was, 'I stopped working years ago. But I might start gloating if it isn't too hard.'

Many of us think that if we won the lottery we'd end up on a beach somewhere, drinking cocktails and being waited on hand and foot. I have to say, it does sound rather nice, doesn't it? But how long could you really keep that up for before you got well and truly bored?

There are many ways to answer this question but your focus must be on showing that you'd intend to make constructive use of your time and don't by any means feel obliged to say that you'd stop working, at least not completely.

EXAMPLE

That's a very interesting question. I assume you're meaning a sufficiently large sum of money that I'd be financially independent for life? Initially, I think I'd take a bit of a career break and perhaps go travelling for a while, not least to give myself some thinking time and time to adjust to my new circumstances. After that, I think I would certainly continue working to a degree but I'd probably aim to work on a not-for-profit basis; for example, volunteer work for a charity. And I'd certainly aim for a better work–life balance. I have many hobbies, such as playing the piano, which I would appreciate having more time to be able to indulge. I'm also very keen to learn Spanish. I think I'd certainly find many ways to occupy my time productively.

Word of warning

Don't venture into the territory of, for example, telling the interviewer just what model of Aston Martin you'd be intending to buy yourself or how you'd quite like a butler to serve your gin and tonic every evening. Restrict your thoughts to ones which show you as someone who needs to continually develop and grow and isn't content to just sit back and rest on their laurels.

38. Can you tell me about the best teacher you ever had?

Alternative and related questions

Who was your favourite teacher and why?

The meaning behind the question

You might think we're definitely into the realm of the amateur psychiatrist here. But are we? What is a teacher, if not an early form of manager or boss? The interviewer will be interested in your explanation as to why you consider this particular teacher to be the best you ever had because it'll give them insight into how you like to be managed and what kind of a person you will be to manage.

Your answer

No one forgets a good teacher. Just take a look at the dedication at the beginning of this book.

This is quite a personal question and so your answer should be personal too. Tell the interviewer in your own words exactly what you feel made this particular teacher so special, taking care to portray yourself as a serious and enthusiastic student.

It's also a good idea to slip into your answer mention of some quality you now possess as a direct result of this teacher. It's an indirect opportunity to blow your own trumpet.

EXAMPLE

For me, the best teacher I ever had was my GCSE History teacher at secondary school. Whilst I find history interesting, it was certainly not one of my favourite subjects. I much prefer mathematics and science. However, through her passion for the subject, she was able to inspire me to become passionate about it too; to see beyond the straight facts and dates and to really see history come to life. She didn't just teach what was on the basic curriculum; she went much further than that. For example, we would plough through old newspaper cuttings and write articles as if we were journalists living and working in the period we were studying. By using unconventional techniques, she really engaged her students and I, consequently, achieved an A grade. Even now, I find the research and analysis techniques she taught me to be very useful in my current line of work.

Word of warning

It should go without saying that you don't want to tell the interviewer that you never liked any of your teachers because they'll just think you have a problem with authority.

39. If you could meet any historical figure, who would it be and why?

Alternative and related questions

If you could meet any personality living or dead, who would it be and why?
Who do you most admire and why?

The meaning behind the question

This question is not quite as nutty as it might sound. If the interviewer can identify what sort of person you admire, it will tell them a lot about your own values.

Your answer

First and foremost, you should obviously select someone who well deserves to be respected and admired, and, ideally, choose someone who has certain characteristics in common with you or with the person you'd like to become; characteristics which you can talk about. Choose someone who has some relevance to your current line of work. I'd quite like to meet Ingrid Bergman but it's hard to see how that could be a relevant and useful choice.

EXAMPLE

Now that's a very interesting question. Let me just think a second . . . I reckon I would like to have been able to meet William Shakespeare. I've always been fascinated by his work. I'd like to know how much of his work he achieved by himself, how much of it was more of a team effort, how he worked with his various collaborators, how the plays evolved over time . . . I know that almost all of his plays were based on earlier sources but I'd still like to know from where he drew his inspiration and how he managed to make them his own. I'm also interested in the business side of things. Whereas a number of his contemporaries might also have achieved critical success at the time, none of them seems to have been nearly as competent as Shakespeare at handling practical matters and business relationships. He ended his life a rich man, rather than dying in poverty like some of his contemporaries. He clearly had a broad diversity of different talents; a very interesting person.

Word of warning

It's best to steer clear of anyone who might be too controversial. This means avoiding political and religious figures as well as anyone whose reputation might have been excessively sullied.

---

40. What are you most afraid of?

Alternative and related questions

What is your greatest fear?
What keeps you up at night?

The meaning behind the question

An inherently negative question really puts you on the spot because, as the interviewer well knows, it's hard for you to wriggle out of. Along the lines of 'What are your weaknesses?' this is a very probing question, which might just dig up some very useful information for the interviewer.

Your answer

Sounds like just the sort of thing a psychiatrist might say, doesn't it? But, no, it's coming from the mouth of an interviewer, so just be sure not to answer as if it was a psychiatrist asking it.

What could you be most afraid of? Failure, cockroaches, using the telephone? Whilst katsaridaphobia and telephonophobia are not suitable answers, atychiphobia might possibly be, although I'd be very wary of baffling the interviewer with words most people have never heard of. In any case, fear of failure might make you sound like an insecure perfectionist or, worse, a defeatist.

Really, the best way to answer this question is to tell the interviewer that there's nothing in particular that you're afraid of, or assuming the interviewer hasn't phrased the question in such a way that it only applies to a work context, you can tell them about a natural, universal human fear, such as the fear of something bad happening to your family or friends, like serious ill health.

If the interviewer continues to press for an answer, which they're only likely to do if they're asking this question in a work context, then try to pick something which isn't too related to your job and try to downplay it as best as you can, subtly weaving into your answer ways in which you combat your fear.

There's really nothing that I'm particularly afraid of. Like most people, I do get somewhat nervous about having to give presentations, probably because it's not something I have to do very often and I've had no formal training in giving presentations. But I'm pretty good at controlling my nerves and focusing on the task in hand and my presentations are normally very well received. I try to bear in mind that you will always feel more nervous than you actually look and that helps me to feel a lot calmer. I also work hard to prepare very thoroughly for presentations. That really helps to boost my confidence.

Money, money, money. The next half a dozen questions deal with this important topic.

41. Why aren't you earning more?

Alternative and related questions

Why aren't you earning more at your age?

Do you think you are being paid enough?

The meaning behind the question

This is a two-pronged attack. The interviewer is putting you under stress with what is obviously a rather awkward and aggressive question, and secondly, they're looking to see how you justify yourself and the career path you have taken.

Your answer

As with other tough questions, it's important to remain calm and not to become defensive.

The best approach is to justify the career decisions you have taken because they have led you to where you are today and put you in a position where you do now expect to earn more than you have done previously.

Turn the question round on them. Go from a question which implies a weakness to an answer which demonstrates your strengths.

EXAMPLE

Rather than focus on short-term earnings, I have been more focused during my career to date on gaining a broad variety of marketable skills and experience. I've been focused on developing within my line of work and have, consequently, deliberately chosen certain jobs not because of the financial package but because of what I would learn from them. I've certainly never changed jobs just because of financial incentives. Training and development opportunities have, to date, always been more important to me. However, I'm not saying that I'm not now very keen to realise my worth. I fully recognise my current market value and achieving a respectable market value is one of my long-term goals.

Word of warning

Without being overly defensive, you should definitely justify your career decisions. Don't let the interviewer trick you into admitting you've made mistakes along the way.

---

42. How much do you think you are really worth?

Alternative and related questions

What salary package are you expecting for this role?

The meaning behind the question

This question is very similar to a question we previously covered in Chapter 3, 'What salary package are you expecting for this role?' But it's not the same. The interviewer isn't directly asking for you to start quoting figures (although you can expect that they're probably just about to); they're asking you to give a statement as to what you feel you're worth and why.

Your answer

This is an excellent opportunity to make a powerful sales pitch to support your case. They've handed you the chance to do this, so you need to make the most of it. This sort of question wouldn't normally crop up until towards the end of an interview, so you should have had plenty of time to get a better handle on what it is that they are looking for and precisely how you can not only meet but surpass their requirements.

It's make-or-break time. Use this question to outline succinctly yet compellingly how it is that you could be of significant worth to their organisation.

EXAMPLE

I feel I have significant worth to a prospective employer and to your organisation in particular. My broad range of experience has enabled me to develop the precise skills you are looking for and I'm a perfect match for the job description you've outlined. Whilst you listed knowledge of German as 'desirable', my German is fluent, and having worked for a few months in Germany, I also have a good understanding of German culture and the way German business operates. As you're intending to start exporting to Germany – clearly a major potential market – I believe I could be a very valuable asset to your organisation. Whilst the salary package on offer won't necessarily be the deciding factor in my choice, I am aware of my value and am naturally keen to be remunerated in a manner which best reflects my worth.

Word of warning

If you work in sales or some other highly money-driven and largely commission-based role then this question is more important than ever. As it's a precursor to discussing precise figures you really do need to make a very strong case.

---

43. How much does money matter to you?

Alternative and related questions

How important is money to you?

If you won the lottery, would you stop working?

The meaning behind the question

No, this question doesn't mean the interviewer is about to make you a derisory salary offer. Although it might not be immediately apparent, this question is actually a close cousin of a question we covered a few pages back, 'If you won the lottery, what would you do?' The interviewer is looking into what your values are; what motivates and drives you.

Your answer

Money is important to pretty much all of us but is it what's most important? Whatever your opinion on the subject it's important not to give the impression that it's all that matters to you. That won't impress the interviewer. Instead, shift the focus to more 'desirable' motivations for you to turn up for work each day instead of staying at home and sitting on the sofa watching TV. And try to make your answer relevant to your current application if at all possible.

EXAMPLE

I think money probably matters to me about as much as it does to anyone. It's obviously vital and necessary for us to live and prosper but, at the same time, it's not my single most important driving force. I see money very much as a means to an end, not an end in itself. Whilst being appropriately and fairly rewarded for the work I do and for what I achieve for an organisation is something that I take seriously, there are many other factors which motivate, drive and inspire me, in particular, the desire to learn and to develop, both professionally and personally. I wouldn't, for example, decide to change jobs purely for financial reasons. There would have to be a number of other positive reasons for me to make such a decision, as there are in the case of the job for which I am now being interviewed. You're offering an interesting and compelling new challenge in a well-regarded organisation with considerable scope for me to progress significantly in my chosen career path.

Word of warning

As with the previous question, if you work in sales or some other highly money-driven and largely commission-based role then this question takes on a particular importance. The example given above probably won't cut the mustard. They'll most likely be looking for more of a killer instinct.

44. Would you still be interested in this job if your current employer offered a pay rise?

Alternative and related questions

Would you still be interested in this job if your current employer offered a promotion?

What will you do if your current employer makes you a counter-offer?

The meaning behind the question

The interviewer is testing again to see how serious you are about moving jobs and what your motivations are in wishing to do so. Is it all just a question of money? Are you potentially wasting their time and likely to subsequently turn down any job offer? Or are you really committed to this new opportunity? Maybe you're just on a fishing trip, trying to get a better idea of your market value or, worse, just getting in some interview practice. Questions like this can easily catch out such candidates.

Your answer

Your employer may well try to encourage you to stay with them, so you need to be prepared to face the possibility that they might offer you an improvement to the salary package they currently offer.

You might well be very tempted to accept such an offer, so it is important to remember your specific reasons for wanting to resign in the first place. Was money really your main motivator?

Whilst I'm not saying you shouldn't give serious consideration to counter-offers – and in some cases accept them – I would say that you should proceed with caution. Be warned that research shows that people who accept such counter-offers normally move on within less than a year anyway. Money is rarely the only motivator.

Moving back to this question, the answer has to be to tell the interviewer that you would indeed remain interested in this job and why.

> **EXAMPLE**
>
> I would most definitely still be interested in this job, even if my current employer did offer me a pay rise. Money is not my only

motivator. Whilst I would obviously have to give their offer some consideration, I would remind myself of the specific reasons for wanting to move on to a new job in the first place and it's more than just a question of money. I'm looking for a new challenge. I'm looking for new opportunities to develop and progress. In short, I'm looking for just the kind of role you are currently offering.

Word of warning

Besides a pay rise, your current employer may even offer you a promotion or a move to a different branch or department. This sort of counter-offer will take more serious thought on your part. How does the new job they are offering compare to the one you are planning to go to?

And be prepared for the interviewer to follow up the question we've just covered with one covering the above-mentioned scenario.

45. Have you ever had to take a pay cut to keep your job?

Alternative and related questions

Have you ever had your pay reduced as an alternative to being made redundant?

Would you take a pay cut to keep your job?

Have you ever left a job because you refused to take a pay cut?

The meaning behind the question

With so much economic turmoil over the past few years, an increasing number of people have indeed taken pay cuts in order to keep their jobs. The interviewer wants to know if this has happened to you and, if so, what the circumstances were and why you accepted. It will tell them a lot about your ability to weigh up options and take tough but necessary decisions for the benefit of long-term goals.

Your answer

If the answer to the question is 'No' then simply say so. There's nothing worth adding.

If you have experienced this say so. I say above that the interviewer wants to know if this 'has happened' to you. Of course, it's not something that 'happens' to anyone; it's something that someone consciously decides. You have a choice. Either you take the pay cut and keep your job or you refuse and you move on. Explain why you chose the former path, taking care to underline your commitment and loyalty to your employer.

EXAMPLE

As my company entered the last recession, it was particularly badly hit financially. It was clear that they couldn't continue as they had been at least in the short term. They considered redundancies, and, after consulting with the staff, we reached agreement that we would all take a 25 per cent pay cut so as to stave off any redundancies, on condition of receiving a degree of equity in the company. I agreed to this because I could see that it was just a short-term situation, I had confidence in my employers and I felt that it was more important to concentrate on the long-term benefits. Staying with the company during the recession taught me a great deal about cost management and how to remain competitive in business even when under signifi-cant financial strain. I gained excellent experience as a result and also ended up with shares in the company, which have now increased sig-nificantly in value.

---

46. Have you ever asked for but been refused a pay rise?

Alternative and related questions

Have you ever been refused a pay rise?

The meaning behind the question

If the interviewer manages to extract a 'Yes' from you then you'd better have a good explanation because otherwise they'll seize the opportunity to pigeonhole you as someone who might overestimate their worth and who could therefore be problematic.

Your answer

If you've never been refused a pay rise then this is a very straightforward question but, if you have, then the trickiest aspect of this question is probably deciding whether to tell the truth or not. Far be it from me to encourage you to lie, but unless you can make a good case which makes your actions appear entirely reasonable, then it may be best just to play it safe and say this has never happened to you, assuming, of course, that there's no way the interviewer could reasonably discover the truth.

'No' remains, in most cases, the best answer to this question. However, I'm going to assume you're an eminently honest person and that you do indeed have a reasonable justification for this having happened to you and I'll give you an example answer accordingly.

> **EXAMPLE**
>
> Yes, I have. In asking for a pay rise, I outlined the progress I had made since I started the role, demonstrating to the HR manager the value I added to the organisation, which, in my opinion, warranted a higher level of remuneration. I gave precise examples to back up and support my claims and I felt I had demonstrated what I was really worth. However, the management decided to decline my request, citing financial problems in the company, and given that I had already been offered another job at that salary level and with good potential for further professional development, I decided it was necessary for me to move on. Sometimes you just have to move on in order to move upwards. I would have been quite happy to stay but, with children to support, I had to take the decision to leave. Having accepted the other offer, my employers did then make a counter-offer but, having committed to the new opportunity, I felt that I had to honour that commitment.

The final questions, just to round things off, cover a few miscellaneous issues such as health, relocation and deal making.

47. Do you have any medical conditions to declare?

Alternative and related questions

Do you have a disability of any sort?
How do you cope with your disability?

The meaning behind the question

No hidden meaning. It's a perfectly reasonable factual question.

Your answer

It is permissible for an employer to question you as to whether or not you have a significant medical condition or disability. However, the Equality Act generally prevents them from taking this into account when making their selection. On this basis, one might wonder why they have the right to ask you at interview and why it can't wait until they have made a firm job offer. The reason is that an employer is only obliged to make 'reasonable adjustments' to accommodate such an employee. If, despite such adjustments, a candidate would still be unable to do the job effectively (as a result of their medical condition or disability) then the employer is allowed to reject their application.

If you do have a medical condition or disability which you should declare then your aim should be to briefly disclose the nature of the issue and then go on to detail what, if any, adjustments would be required for you to undertake the role.

Whilst it is uncommon for an employer to discriminate on the basis of a medical condition or disability, they may have concerns as to the changes they will need to make. If you are aware of state funding which may be available to support such changes, then you can go a long way towards assuaging such fears. You should also reassure them that, subject to these changes, you will be able to undertake the role just as effectively as anyone else.

I am partially deaf in my left ear but I wear a very discreet hearing aid in that ear and this effectively resolves the problem. No adjustments would be required on your part to accommodate this minor disability. As you can see from my CV, it has no impact on my ability to get the job done.

Word of warning

Don't make the mistake of thinking that the interviewer is asking the question we covered in Chapter 4, 'What's your sickness record like?' That's definitely not the same question as this one.

48. Why do you want to relocate?

Alternative and related questions

For what reasons does the idea of relocation appeal to you?

The meaning behind the question

There's nothing sneaky about this question. The interviewer just wants to establish what your motivations are in being prepared to relocate for this job and to get some insight into your decision-making processes, i.e. they want to establish that you really have thought through this issue.

Your answer

So why do you want to relocate? Is it just because this job is an opportunity too good to be missed? Is it because relocating will take you closer to certain family or friends? Has your spouse/partner perhaps had to relocate to the same destination? Maybe it's because you have children and you want them to be closer to better schools/the countryside/the seaside. There are many possible reasons why you might wish to relocate.

But there's only one correct answer to this question and that's to explain that your primary reason for relocating is because of the fantastic opportunity you feel this job represents. You can go on to support this with other reasons if appropriate. But your main goal is to demonstrate to the interviewer your enthusiasm for the role for which you are applying.

EXAMPLE

I principally want to locate because of the excellent opportunity I feel this role within your organisation represents. I am very interested in the role and believe that it warrants my relocation. In this respect alone, the benefits outweigh any possible downside. Furthermore, my sister and her family live in Hampshire and I'd certainly like to move to be closer to them and I'd also like for my children to be closer to them too. There are also some very good local schools. I've given it a good deal of thought, but everything points towards it being the right decision.

Word of warning

Don't say anything which might lead them to believe that you're only relocating because you feel it's being forced on you. Ensure you portray it as a positive decision on your part.

---

49. Can you perceive any problems in relocating?

Alternative and related questions

Are you willing to relocate if necessary?
Are you willing to go where the organisation sends you?

The meaning behind the question

This could be a reasonably straightforward factual question if relocation is an obvious prerequisite for the job. On the other hand, if no mention has previously been made of relocation then either the organisation has failed to communicate effectively or the interviewer is trying to put you on the spot again.

Your answer

If you're aware of the need to relocate in order to undertake this new job then your answer just needs to cover that fact and to emphasise that you're fully prepared and ready for this and that you certainly don't perceive it causing any problems. If you can, mention a previous instance where you've had to relocate for a new job (or whilst working for another organisation). If not, then just say you've thought the matter through carefully and you're entirely happy with the prospect.

If this is the first time you've heard mention of the possibility of relocation then your answer is somewhat trickier. First of all, you should point out that this is the first you've heard of it and then you should go on to explain that it's something you would be prepared to consider. It may be that there's no way you would ever contemplate relocating but telling the interviewer this is going to weaken your case, regardless of whether they are seriously requiring you to relocate or not. Remember that if you are required to relocate but you decide you really don't want to, then you can simply turn down their offer of a job. But your first priority is to actually make sure you get an offer.

EXAMPLE

I haven't actually been previously made aware that relocation was a possibility. It hasn't been mentioned to me. However, it's something that I would be prepared to consider. This role within your organisation is very appealing and, if offered the job, I may well decide that it would warrant relocating. It would of course depend on your offer and on the precise circumstances. Can you tell me a little bit more about this issue of relocation, please? I can then give it some further thought.

50. How would you react if I were to offer you this job on the spot?

Alternative and related questions

What would you say if I were to offer you this job immediately?

What would be your answer if I were to offer you this job now?

The meaning behind the question

This is an interesting question which interviewers can use to test your decision-making and deal-brokering skills. The interview is a potential business transaction. You're discussing the possibility of a long-term deal. It just happens that you're the product. The way you answer this question will give the interviewer some insight into how you might handle future such negotiations when you are, for example, dealing with a potential supplier.

Your answer

No, you're not going to jump up and kiss them. They're not saying that they are going to offer you this job on the spot; they're just asking how you would react if they did.

There are two main possible answers to this question. You may say that you'd accept their offer immediately or you may say that you'd need a little more information first and would need a little time to consider their offer. I would vouch for the latter. I'm not saying you shouldn't reiterate your interest in the post, but unless they've already outlined the precise details of their offer, including the important question of salary, then it's only reasonable and sensible that you will want to have that information first and require some time to consider your options. They should respect you for this.

There is a third possibility. You may have decided by now that this job isn't the right one for you and now that you have mastered interview technique (hopefully with a little help from me) there are other, better options out there for you. But I'd avoid saying that you'd turn down their offer; at least wait to see if you actually get an offer. At the very least, you can then use this offer to help you when negotiating any other offers you may receive.

EXAMPLE

I'd be very pleased. I am definitely very interested in this role and in your organisation. However, before formally accepting, I would need to see the precise terms of your offer so as to see how it compares to other offers I have received, and I'd subsequently need a little time to think over my various options and decide which one I should be pursuing. It's an important decision and obviously not something I should be in a rush to make. But, if you'd like to make me an offer, then I'll obviously give it my serious consideration.

Your ideas wanted!

We've now covered a very broad variety of possible questions and in some depth. However, I'm always very interested in new, unusual, weird and wacky or particularly difficult interview questions. I'm talking about the kind of question you're unlikely to find covered in any books on interview questions.

If you have been asked a particular question in the past that surprised you, shocked you, stunned you or that you really struggled with, then please send me an email (**james.innes@jamesinnes.com**), and who knows, you may well find your question featured in the next edition of this book and a free copy of that new edition in the post to you.

Most people have at least one interview question they've been asked which they will end up remembering for the rest of their lives. For me it was the interviewer who asked me, 'Can you make tea?' I look forward to hearing what it was for you.

Chapter **6**

Twenty weird
and wonderful
questions: prepare
to be surprised!

1. See this pen? Can you sell it to me?

Alternative and related questions

See this pencil/paperclip/computer/desk/mobile phone/shoe . . .

The meaning behind the question

You might think this question is only likely to be asked if you work in sales but you'd be wrong. It can be asked of almost anyone, regardless of whether sales skills are important to their job. It's a question which forces a candidate to think on their feet whilst under pressure, and this can tell an interviewer a lot about a candidate, not least how clearly they are able to think and to communicate. It's a classic question, which regularly features in interviews.

Your answer

There are two possible ways of answering this question depending on your line of work. If you do work in sales then you shouldn't need too much advice from me as to how to handle the question. You simply need to demonstrate your standard sales patter and techniques to the interviewer, inventing pricing, discount offers, payment terms etc. as you go. The precise details are not important; it's the methods you employ which count; identifying the customer's needs and matching those to the specific benefits of the product etc.

If, on the other hand, you don't work in sales (which is the majority of us) then this question is going to be a little trickier to handle. Don't let yourself be panicked, though; the interviewer knows full well that you are not used to selling and they won't be expecting you to have a whole arsenal of sales techniques at your disposal. And don't take yourself too seriously; good people are always light-hearted and friendly.

Concentrate on:

➤ talking the interviewer into expressing a need – or needs;

➤ describing the object, including both its features and its benefits;

➤ discussing pricing (which you will invent off the top of your head);

➤ asking them directly for the sale.

> **EXAMPLE**
>
> I'm sure you'll agree with me that a pen is vital to your day-to-day work and it's, therefore, important to make sure you've got just the right one. This pen is solidly constructed so as to be durable for everyday use, even if it rolls off your desk onto the floor. It has a plentiful ink reserve so there's less chance of the pen running dry at a critical moment. It fits comfortably into the hand and even has a clip so you can safely attach it to your jacket pocket when you're on the move. I can offer you this pen at the very reasonable price of 20 pence. However, if you were to take three – I'm sure your colleagues would also be interested – then I could offer you a 20 per cent discount, making a total of just 48 pence. How many would you like?

Word of warning

It is important to convince the interviewer that your answer is not rehearsed. If they can clearly identify that you have planned, prepared and rehearsed for this question then it's going to take a whole lot of impact out of your answer.

2. If you were an animal at the zoo, which animal would you be and why?

Alternative and related questions

If you were a dog, what breed of dog would you be?
If you were a biscuit, what type of biscuit would you be?
What type of ice cream are you?
If you were a make of car, what make would you be?
If you were a fruit, what fruit would you be?
Which dinosaur would you like to be?

The meaning behind the question

Clearly the interviewer fancies themselves as a bit of an amateur psychiatrist. Superficially, it's a fairly silly question; however, the answers candidates give can be very revealing. The interviewer is obviously testing your ability to think on your feet, but they are also looking for some further insight into how you perceive yourself.

Your answer

This is definitely one of the most difficult questions to answer. You've got to quickly think of all the different possible animals (or dog breeds or cars etc.) and then pick one which has certain positive characteristics which you feel match your own. You've then got to explain your choice to the interviewer. This isn't easy but don't panic; stall for time if necessary. And remember that there is no correct answer to the question; it's all about how you reach your answer and how you express yourself.

EXAMPLE

I can't say anyone has ever asked me that before! If I could just have a second to think about it. Right, the chimpanzee springs to mind. They're a lot like humans really. They work together as a team, cooperate with each other for the benefit of the whole group, are sensitive to each other socially and they always seem to have a good sense of fun and humour. I'm also rather fond of bananas!

---

3. If there was a monkey hanging from a chandelier, how would you get it down?

Alternative and related questions

If there was a venomous snake sunbathing on your patio, how would you get rid of it?

If a hippo falls in a hole, how would you get it out?

The meaning behind the question

We're clearly getting into the weird and wacky with this question but interviewers have been known to ask such questions. You might think you'll never get asked such a seemingly ridiculous question in an interview, however, I can personally vouch that questions like this do get asked, having been asked precisely this question myself many years ago, although it was admittedly for a scholarship interview rather than a job interview.

Your answer

There is no right answer to this type of question. It is purely a test of your ability to analyse a problem and identify possible solutions. Once you realise this you will hopefully be a lot less rattled by the question than I was at what was virtually my first-ever interview. Don't let yourself be rattled by the question, and don't lose your sense of humour either; telling the interviewer you'd probably get your rifle out is unlikely to go down well.

EXAMPLE

Interesting question! I suppose there are a number of possible solutions to this problem. It's a case of identifying these possible solutions and selecting the one which has the best chance of success. The most obvious idea which springs to my mind is to try to entice it down by offering it a banana. Alternatively, I could try to scare it down. Shouting at it would probably make it even less likely to come down, but flicking the light switch on and off might work. Spraying water at it might also convince him to budge but there's perhaps too much risk of collateral damage. Failing that, I think I'd find the monkey's owner or keeper and I'd delegate the task to them.

---

4. Why don't polar bears eat penguins?

Alternative and related questions

Why do butterflies generally come out during the day and moths generally come out at night?
Is a tomato a vegetable?

The meaning behind the question

This is actually a general knowledge question. Polar bears don't eat penguins because polar bears live in the Arctic and penguins live in the Antarctic. In asking this sort of question, the interviewer doesn't really expect many people to get the right answer and they don't necessarily care too much if they do. They're more interested in how you think your answer through. So unless you know the correct answer, this question is similar to the previous question.

Your answer

Because they can't get the wrappers off. Well, that would certainly be one possible answer. Let's face it, you're probably not a zoologist and this is one occasion where demonstrating a sense of humour – not to mention some lateral thinking – wouldn't do you any harm. I certainly know of at least one candidate who answered in this fashion. However, assuming you don't know the correct answer nor are a budding comedian, the best answer to give is along the same lines as the previous question; demonstrate your ability to analyse the situation and identify possible theories.

EXAMPLE

I'm afraid I'll have to admit that biology isn't one of my strong points. I do enjoy watching documentaries, but I haven't seen one yet which would give me the answer to this question. I can think of a number of possible hypotheses: maybe penguins are too small for a polar bear to bother with and they stick to larger prey, maybe polar bears aren't fast enough to catch a penguin, perhaps there's something toxic about penguins – some form of defence mechanism, maybe polar bears live and hunt inland but penguins spend most of their time in the water or at the water's edge. I obviously don't know for sure but these would be my possible ideas. Am I close?

---

5. How much water would it take to fill St Paul's Cathedral?

Alternative and related questions

How many bottles of red wine are drunk in France on Christmas Day?
How many basketballs can you fit in this room?
How many bricks are there in the world?
How many planes fly over London every day?
How long would it take to wash all the windows of the Shard?

The meaning behind the question

This is definitely not a general knowledge question. It is a question specifically designed to test your reasoning skills. The interviewer wants to see how you approach the problem, how able you are to identify the relevant factors and, having identified the relevant factors, how you use them to calculate your answer. They're not expecting you to be able to give them a precise figure. They're mainly looking to see how you rise to the challenge of attempting to formulate an answer.

Your answer

You'd be forgiven for pausing for a second to think your answer through. This is most definitely not an easy question. Try to keep a clear head and identify what factors will lead you to an answer. You're not expected to be an expert on St Paul's Cathedral nor on French wine-drinking habits. The key is to try to think through the question logically and to convey your thoughts to the interviewer in an ordered fashion.

> **EXAMPLE**
>
> That's a difficult question. If we assume that we have already plugged up any potential leaks then the answer primarily hinges on a precise calculation of the internal volume of St Paul's Cathedral. I don't know St Paul's Cathedral very well but I know it's a complicated piece of architecture. In order to answer the question reasonably precisely I'd need to see plans of the building so that I could break it up into a number of different shapes, measure them and calculate their volumes accordingly. I'd also have to make a deduction for interior furniture etc., although I would expect that to be fairly minor.

If your work involves having to handle complex calculations of this nature then you might want to take your answer to the next level by actually having a stab at the correct figure.

At a guess, I'd say St Paul's is roughly 200 m long, 50 m wide and 50 m high making a total of half a million cubic metres. Features such as the dome will add to this figure but internal furnishings, pillars and walls will reduce it. With 1,000 litres in a cubic metre, half a million cubic metres equates to 500 million litres. Without more precise data that would be my best estimate. Seeing the plans of the building would be useful but another technique would be to buy a scale model from a souvenir shop or suchlike. I could then determine an upper limit by plugging any leaks, placing it in water, measuring how much water it displaced and then scaling this figure up.

Word of warning

Don't make the mistake of asking what the correct answer is. The interviewer probably won't know and you might just make them feel a little foolish!

6. Who would win in a fight between Superman and Batman?

Alternative and related questions

Who would you rather be locked in a small room with: Darth Vader or Hannibal Lecter?

The meaning behind the question

This question has actually been around for some time and is in no way a reference to the 2016 feature film *Batman v Superman: Dawn of Justice*! In common with many of these types of question, the interviewer may have run out of questions but, more likely, they have just decided to throw one weird one in there to see how you react. It is just possible that your answer might allow your personality under stress to come through, so do be aware of that. Fortunately, it is highly unlikely that you will be asked more than one such question!

Your answer

The answer is unlikely to make a difference to whether you get the job or not unless you really mess it up completely! So my advice is to stay calm and take a little time by repeating the question back. If you have an opinion then calmly state that. If, on the other hand, you haven't a clue then explain that your usual approach when faced with something you don't know the answer to is to take some time to think about it so you can come back with a properly thought through answer rather than a kneejerk one, which might be the wrong one. And remember to smile or the interviewer will think you have absolutely no sense of humour!

EXAMPLE

That's a good question. Who would win in a fight between Superman and Batman? I think Batman as, although Superman has superhuman powers and can overcome many challenges, I remember watching Batman's fighting skills and they're really rather impressive. Where he lacks in strength he makes up for with technique! Then, of course, Superman can fly . . . It's a tough one. I guess I'll just have to watch the film!

---

7. Who is your favourite Doctor Who?

Alternative and related questions

Who is your favourite James Bond actor?
Which is your favourite boy band?

The meaning behind the question

A simple amateur psychologist type of question, which might not be quite so simple to answer! The interviewer is expecting (hoping?) your answer will reveal something of your personality.

Your answer

Do you even have a favourite Doctor Who? Can you even name one at all?! I can only think of one, Jon Pertwee. So how would I answer this question? With difficulty! How can I have a favourite when I can only think of one? Well, I'd suggest honesty. Honesty, in interviews, is (almost) always the best policy.

Of course, if you are fortunate enough to have a favourite Doctor Who then say so and explain why. Just try not to sound too much of a geek!

EXAMPLE

I'm sorry but I'll have to admit I don't know very much about Doctor Who. I can only think of one, Jon Pertwee. So I really can't claim to have a favourite, I'm afraid. I could tell you who my favourite James Bond actor is though!

---

8. Is a Jaffa Cake a cake or a biscuit?

Alternative and related questions

Is Coca-Cola the only real cola drink?
Apple or Microsoft, which would you use for your business?

The meaning behind the question

We assume here that the organisation hasn't got a vacancy in the Trivial Pursuit league! This typical 'tricky trivia' question looks more like something you would discuss over a cup of tea in the staff room, but for an interviewer, it's another way of checking the candidate's ability to look at a situation from different sides and weigh up arguments before making a decision. It also examines impartiality and can give a good steer on how rational a candidate is able to be.

Using the Jaffa Cake is not as far-fetched as it can seem either. There was in fact a court ruling in this matter in 1991, when the Jaffa Cake manufacturer McVitie's and Her Majesty's Revenue and Customs ended up in a tribunal over whether Jaffa Cake was a cake (exempt from VAT payment) or a biscuit (VAT would have to be paid). The Jaffa guys won the court case, so it's a cake, at least from a tax point of view!

Your answer

As usual, do not panic! Depending how wide your knowledge of trivia is, you might even be aware of that court case. But it's probably unlikely. So you need to demonstrate the different arguments and then make your choice accordingly. It really doesn't matter whether you are right or not. It's how you arrive at your answer which counts. In a nutshell, this is an exercise in putting forward arguments from two different sides and then making an informed decision.

EXAMPLE

It's a cake, just as in the name. You wouldn't call something a cake if it wasn't a cake, would you? And it's soft, just like a cake. They are just next to the biscuits in the shops but that's more down to the shape, not the content. It is still basically a sponge cake with some orange marmalade on top so it can't just be a biscuit. I also left one out on a plate the other day and it went hard just like a cake!

Word of warning

You may think you can get away scot-free by claiming you have never heard of Jaffa Cakes, but your interviewer will probably then give you a detailed description of them and ask you to proceed anyway! (By the way, Wikipedia describes Jaffa Cakes as 'biscuit-shaped, circular, 2½ inches (64 mm) in diameter [with] three layers: a sponge base, a layer of orange flavoured jelly and a coating of chocolate' . . .)

---

9. Do you like to sing in the bath?

Alternative and related questions

What music do you listen to in the car?
Eurovision Song Contest or X Factor?

The meaning behind the question

Again, a question like this is not likely to make or break your chances of getting the job – unless you allow it to! The interviewer may hope your answer might give some insight into your personality/sense of humour and, who knows, perhaps your out-of-work interests.

Your answer

Your answer definitely should NOT include any reference to showering, bathing or anything too personal. And you might want to avoid expressing some definite musical tastes if they are likely to be controversial or provoke a negative response. If you like, for example, songs from musicals or Country and Western perhaps keep your preferences to yourself, appreciating that not everyone will be a fan. Essentially, stick to safe ground!

> **EXAMPLE**
>
> Yes! Sometimes. I like singing. I like a good ballad. They may not be to everyone's taste but I enjoy them and no one hears me anyway! Singing helps me to relax and clear my head and that's obviously very important.

10. Which three celebrities would you like to join you for a night out?

Alternative and related questions

Who would you like to be left on a desert island with?

If you had to choose one, which famous person would you invite to your wedding?

The meaning behind the question

This is really quite similar to Question 39 back in Chapter 5: If you could meet any historical figure, who would it be and why? But it's more dangerous than that one! It gives you much greater scope to make yourself look silly! Often labelled a 'personality-probing' question, this sort of question is a light-hearted way for the interviewer to find out a little about your approach to life and what you value. The interviewer is likely to be interested in whatever choices you make as long as you justify them in positive terms giving sensible reasons why you would choose them.

Let's begin with how not to answer this question: If you feel tempted to list terrorists, serial killers or models as your three celebrities as a joke, then please refrain. Instead, let the nature of the job you're applying for the personal qualities, professional requirements and what you know about the organisation determine your choice of celebs. Think of three areas that are important for the role and then think of a suitable celebrity for each. This sort of question is not easy to do on the hoof, but the chances are that you have thought about this before at some stage. Just make sure you carefully justify your selection. And you can even choose three people who are closely linked to each other; for example, the Queen, Prince Charles and Prince William! There isn't a rule which says you have to choose three people from totally different walks of life.

EXAMPLE

One of the people I admire most and who also seems very outgoing and approachable is Sir Richard Branson. There must be so much one could learn from him. I am also a huge sports fan and have always been interested in how successful managers work with their teams. Chelsea's manager, José Mourinho, could undoubtedly share some tips on how I can drive the sales team forward, and if he's in a good mood he can be really funny. I would also invite Jamie Oliver as he's not only a great entrepreneur and an easygoing guy but if we decide to stay in rather than go out, then he can do the cooking for us!

---

11. What would you do if the sun died out?

Alternative and related questions

What would you do if the world ended?
What would you do if time stopped?

The meaning behind the question

Yes, at first sight, it does sound like an utterly ridiculous question. But I will admit to believing this to be one of the best interview questions ever. Because it really is a very hard one to answer and also reveals an awful lot about the candidate; their general knowledge, their ability to think on their feet, their powers of reasoning, their sense of humour etc.

Your answer

Well, the bad news is that you'd probably die out too! Without the sun, most life on Earth would disappear pretty rapidly, including the vast majority, if not all, of mankind. Would any humans survive? Well, some surely could for a while but not indefinitely. And, unless you're Barack Obama, you're probably going to be one of those who won't last more than a week.

But what is meant by 'died out'? Does it simply stop shining? Does it vanish completely (with obvious gravitational repercussions)? As it happens, it's theoretically impossible for the sun to just stop shining or to vanish. When the sun actually dies, in the sense of burning up all of its Hydrogen fuel supply, it will take the Earth with it. In fact, life on Earth will be destroyed well before the sun first expands into a red giant (swallowing up the whole planet) before finally collapsing into a white dwarf because we've only got about another billion years to go before all the water on the planet evaporates as the sun becomes just 10% brighter than it is at present. But, hey, you can get a lot done in a billion years!

EXAMPLE

I would think that if the sun died out then I'd probably die out too! I think it'd just be a matter of time. It depends on what precisely you mean by 'died out'. But, generally speaking, without the sun, life on Earth would be very severely compromised and especially so for *Homo sapiens*. It'd be a good time to be a microorganism living in the Earth's crust, I reckon!

12. What do you do when there is no answer?

Alternative and related questions

What do you do when you don't know the answer?

The meaning behind the question

This is a Microsoft question. And the answer to this forms the basis for many of the tough questions that you may be faced with where either there is no answer or you just can't think of it on the spur of the moment! This question is easier as it allows you to explain clearly your own approach to problem-solving. The interviewer will be interested in your approach and may well ask you to illustrate your answer with an example from your work experience.

Your answer

The interviewer will want to discover your approach to simple problems that require an immediate response and to a problem that is not so urgent but harder to solve. You need to show that you can cope when instant answers are needed but are not so impulsive when you have more time. If you can think of a situation in the workplace that demonstrates how you went about solving a problem that initially didn't have an answer, then this is the time to bring it up.

EXAMPLE

I think there is always an answer, even if some are difficult to find or implement. I'd like to think I was good in a crisis and would try to find an answer taking into account all the information that was available to me at the time. If I had more time then I would consult others and do some research to see if I could come up with some other options. For example, in my current role we had a situation where nobody knew the answer. But by discussing with my colleagues and doing some online research, we came up with a viable and practical solution. I can elaborate on that if you wish?

---

13. How many dogs in the world have the exact same number of hairs?

Alternative and related questions

How many birds in the world have the exact same number of feathers?
How many fish in the world have the exact same number of scales?

The meaning behind the question

A real interview question posed by Capital Asset Exchange & Trading. Yes, some interviewers are just too clever for their own good, and this type of impossible-to-answer question is clearly designed to rattle you. So don't let it!

Your answer

If you don't know the answer (did I say it was impossible to answer? Well, that may have been an exaggeration . . .), then you simply need to retain your composure and use the politicians' old trick of admitting you don't know but not actually saying so in so many words!

As it happens, there is an answer of sorts . . . If you plotted a statistical distribution graph of all the dogs in the world then there is going to be a range of number of hairs that all dogs have; for example, all dogs will have more than 100,000 hairs and less than 20 million. Within that range, given how many dogs there are in the world, there will inevitably be many dogs that have the same number of hairs. OK, so that's not a precise answer, but it is a precise methodology and one which will undoubtedly impress the interviewer.

EXAMPLE

I'd like to give you an answer but, unsurprisingly, I don't have enough data to hand to do so with any great accuracy. I'd need to know the minimum, maximum and average number of hairs and also how many dogs there are in the world. Even then, it would inevitably be an approximation. But, given how many dogs there are in the world, I'd say that plenty of them have the exact same number of hairs as another dog somewhere else in the world.

14. How do you fit a giraffe in a fridge?

Alternative and related questions

How many hippos can you fit into a Mini?
How do you get a gorilla out of a fridge?

The meaning behind the question

As asked in real interviews by UBS. Answering this type of question is very much about showing your mental agility and flexibility. The interviewer wants to hear the reasoning behind your answer and how you reach your conclusion. A nightmare for some, but quite fun for others!

Your answer

There are in fact several ways of answering this question which will be perfectly acceptable to the interviewer. As always, take a deep breath, and although it may seem absurd, try to approach the question logically. You can begin by asking the interviewer:

Is it a baby giraffe or is it fully grown?
How big is the fridge?
Does the giraffe need to be alive once it's in the fridge?
What tools do I have at my disposal?

This, like the previous question, will show the interviewer that you recognise the first step in solving a problem is to establish the facts before you make any decisions or draw any conclusions. Considering the possible answers to these questions, you could conclude that it is perfectly possible to fit the giraffe alive in to either a very large fridge or, if no longer alive, into a smaller one!

> **EXAMPLE**
>
> If it was a baby giraffe, it didn't need to be alive once it was in the fridge and it was a big enough fridge then, assuming had the necessary tools to hand, I'd just need to cut it up, I think! I'd rather not, though; I'm not Ernest Hemingway!

15. How many ways can you get a needle out of a haystack?

Alternative and related questions

How many ways can you find a lost ring on a sandy beach?

The meaning behind the question

Yes, another real question this time from Macquarie Bank. It tests your general knowledge of science as well as your common sense, and ability to think big, remain level-headed and not to be thrown by the question. By the way, no one's expecting you to get this type of question 100% right!

Your answer

As you now know, don't be phased by the weird and wacky nature of the question; it doesn't demand a weird and wacky response. Instead you should knuckle down to some logical thinking here.

To begin with, abandon the idea of actually just looking for the needle within the haystack. Instead, think of how technology and science and some chutzpah could help you out. What would happen if you burned the haystack down? What if there was a storm? What about using water? Magnetism? What if all the hay was eaten? There may be several other methods as well; use your imagination!

EXAMPLE

Quite a few! I could try a really large magnet to pull the needle out. I could also get hold of a wind machine and blow the hay away. Or get a large water tank, put the hay in it and I'd find the needle at the bottom. Or burn it and sift through the ashes. If I had plenty of time, I could guide a herd of cows to the haystack and have them eat the lot, then wait for the needle to emerge or one cow to collapse! Then there's always the possibility of using a metal detector.

16. Would you rather fight a horse-sized duck or 100 duck-sized horses?

Alternative and related questions

Would you rather be attacked by 100 *Tyrannosaurus rex* the size of hamsters or one hamster the size of a *Tyrannosaurus rex*?

The meaning behind the question

And the credit for this fiendish little question apparently goes to BHP Billiton. And fiendish it certainly is. Not to mention famous. (Or is that infamous?) Boris was asked it. Obama has been asked it. This question has become somewhat of a celebrity! The meaning behind it, I personally think, reveals more about the interviewer than anything else!

Your answer

There is no correct answer. But there is a right response! As so often with these weird and wonderful questions it's all about thinking clearly, logically and rationally and doing so under pressure. Technically, a horse-sized duck would be unable to fly, unlikely to be able to walk and would probably have great difficulty even breathing! And a duck-sized horse would have its own problems. So you'd probably win the fight regardless!

EXAMPLE

I'd rather fight a horse-sized duck. The smaller horses get the more obstinate, intractable and wilful they are. Duck-sized ones would be really quite formidable. So I'd much rather just fight a very big duck!

17. If you were an elephant, what would you do with your trunk?

Alternative and related questions

If you were a rhino, what would you do with your horn?
What's the worst thing about being a pair of sunglasses?

The meaning behind the question

Many thanks to Google for this one! Designed to test your creative thinking, this is a 'weird classic' that you can take as seriously as you want to – or not . . . The interviewer does not really want to know about the various different possible usages of elephants' trunks, but, instead, just wants to see if you're going to let yourself be thrown by the question and fall silent, which would especially not be recommended if the position you're being interviewed for requires a creative thinker!

Your answer

There are no incorrect answers to this question. Just try to relax and think of what you could do professionally in the role you're applying for if you had a trunk - like an extra arm, perhaps? Again, having a little think about your CV, the specification for the role and the industry you're in should inspire you to come up with some great ideas!

EXAMPLE

As an executive PA, one is always juggling hundreds of tasks at the same time! I like to stay on top of everything I do, so having a trunk would be a godsend! I could do my administration twice as fast, and with hands-free phone technology I could be on the phone organising events, sending invoices and tweeting all at the same time! It could be a little awkward when I have to meet and greet clients, but if it was retractable and you could put it away when you wanted to then I think everyone would want one!

BLOOPER!

∙∙∙

One of the most entertaining answers I have heard to this question is, "It'd be very useful for doing up my swimsuit or for undoing my dresses. I wouldn't need my husband anymore!" But is that really a 'blooper' or is it actually rather a clever little answer? It certainly shows original and creative thinking – not to mention a sense of humour!

18. What shapes are best for manholes?

Alternative and related questions

Why are manholes circular?
What aren't manhole covers square?
Describe the action of a corkscrew on a cork.

The meaning behind the question

Another seemingly irrelevant question that, on the surface, appears whacky but is, in fact, albeit slightly different, an opportunity for the interviewer to test the candidate's ability to structure an answer and apply logical reasoning. These type of questions were initially used when interviewing candidates for positions within technical sectors, such as computer programming and engineering, but have become increasingly popular when hiring staff for any positions where analytical skills, logical thinking and problem solving is key to the role.

As with similar questions, it is not so much about getting the answer absolutely right, but more about taking a step-by-step, logical approach. You will want to think out loud when you give the answer, so the interviewer can follow your thought-pattern, so these type of answers can be a little long-winded and detailed but that's what the interviewer wants.

Your answer

Most manhole covers are, obviously, round, so your answer should be exploring and comparing other shapes. You may want to think about the practical aspects of handling a manhole cover if you had to work with them yourself: moving them, placing them correctly over the hole etc. You can also consider what could go wrong when handling the cover. What if it was accidentally dropped? Could it fall into the hole? If you then start comparing different shapes: circular, square, triangular, hexagonal, you're likely to see that whoever designed them in the first place knew what they were doing! Mind you, you'd be surprised how good a manhole cover an equilateral triangle would make . . . They're just rather difficult to roll!

EXAMPLE

Well, most manhole covers are round, aren't they? So the chances are that that is the best shape. The question is: Why? If I had to work with them on a daily basis then I would like them to be as practical to handle as possible. I guess that if I had to replace them as part of my job, I would prefer a round one that I could lift off my truck and then roll over to the hole, rather than having to need a colleague to help me carry it. I would also like the workplace to be safe, so if one was dropped near the hole and I was inside it, I would like to know it couldn't fall down through the hole and hit me. A square shape can fall into a square hole diagonally, so the round one would be safer. When my job was done, I would like the cover to fit back easily and round shapes always fit and can be screwed tight and locked by turning them so, yes, it seems that round is best

---

19. Why is water tasteless?

Alternative and related questions

Why doesn't air smell?

The meaning behind the question

Questions like this originally came on the scene in the 1990s and were mainly used when hiring software staff for large multinationals like Apple. But they've spread like wildfire and you could now be asked a question like this in pretty much any interview. Besides testing your ability to think clearly and logically, this question does also involve an element of general knowledge.

Your answer

'The natural substance water per se tends to be tasteless,' wrote Aristotle. Pure, pH-neutral water is not salty, sour, sweet or bitter and it's certainly not umami! Neither does it have any smell, since it is the solvent which your body uses to dissolve other molecules so that you can then smell them. Water makes up the majority of the human body. Do you know the taste of your own tongue? Hard to taste something you're made of! Of course, most of the water we drink actually has various impurities in it, which we can taste, hence the success of bottled water. But now we're getting pernickety, nevertheless, there's nothing to stop you from pointing that out to the interviewer.

EXAMPLE

Well, I believe that water does have a certain taste and people who buy bottled water must agree! As we are largely made of water, we're no doubt not sensitive to the taste of the water but, instead, the various minerals and, sometimes, salts, that bottled water contains. Or other impurities that tap water contains. London tap water certainly isn't tasteless! I'm not saying it's exactly tasty either, though.

20. You have 12 visually identical marbles. They are all the same weight except for two, one of which is lighter than the others and one of which is heavier. You have some good old-fashioned weighing scales (the kind which act on a pivot), which you are permitted to use up to three times at the most. How do you identify which are the heavier and lighter ones?

Alternative and related questions

You have a blob of plasticine whose weight, which is a whole number of grams, you need to find using balancing scales. If the blob weighs up to 100g, what is the minimum number of weights you need to measure it?

If you could fold a piece of paper in half a hundred times, how thick would it be?

The meaning behind the question

This is, quite evidently, a mathematics question, and fortunately for the non-mathematicians, you are only likely to be asked this if you can reasonably be expected to have a sufficient grasp of mathematics either to know or to deduce the answer!

Your answer

The answer, if written, is really rather long. And it's definitely beyond the scope of this book. If you're curious then I suggest you Google it! Actually, whilst one can write the answer out long-hand, I personally think the best way to arrive at it is using a flowchart . . . And the mathematicians amongst you will understand that!

Chapter **7**

Ending the interview: your own questions

Interviews are always a two-way process. Not preparing your own questions for the end of an interview is a common and significant interview mistake.

There aren't many interviews that conclude without the candidate being asked, 'Do you have any questions for me/us?' Almost all interviewers will give you a chance to ask questions and you should use this as an opportunity to further demonstrate your interest and enthusiasm. If you don't then you'll come across as passive and uninterested.

STATISTIC

A recent survey showed that 29 per cent of recruiters stated that the candidate not asking questions or asking poor questions at the end of the interview was sufficient reason for them to 'fail' the candidate.

What to ask

Don't ask too many questions; you're the interviewee, not the interviewer! But be prepared with a few intelligent questions. Here's a good selection of examples for you:

➤ What are the top priorities for my first six months in the job?
➤ What would you expect from me in my first 100 days on the job?
➤ In what ways does this role impact on the growth of the organisation?
➤ How has this role evolved since it was created?
➤ How would you describe the team I will be working with?
➤ How would you describe the work culture here?
➤ What do you enjoy most about working here?
➤ How do you see my role evolving over the next two to three years?
➤ How do you see the organisation evolving over the next five years?
➤ Are there any plans for expansion?
➤ How does the organisation measure its success?
➤ In what ways is performance measured?
➤ What training and professional development opportunities will be available?
➤ What scope is there for future promotion?

You will notice that I have phrased these questions as if you had already bagged the job. It's a subtle psychological technique, which will project self-confidence and help further persuade the interviewer that you are the right candidate for the job.

One last sales pitch

If you have not been asked about something which you feel illustrates an important aspect of your ability to do the job, don't be afraid to bring it up yourself at the end of the interview. You could, for example, ask how important such-and-such an ability is to the job. When the interviewer answers that it is indeed important they've given you the perfect opportunity to roll out a pre-prepared example demonstrating that you have this ability.

An 'advanced' technique

Another good question to ask is whether or not the interviewer has any reservations about your application and if so, what they are. It takes a bit of nerve to ask this question and you had better make jolly sure you are ready to address any reservations they may have; this will probably be your last chance to do so.

It might be described as an 'advanced' technique but if you can uncover any possible objections the interviewer might have to hiring you – and counter-attack effectively – then it can make all the difference. At the very least it's a question which will certainly demonstrate your self-confidence.

BLOOPER!

Don't ask questions just for the sake of it. One candidate, when asked if she had any questions, replied, 'Are you going anywhere nice on your holidays this summer?' Clearly that didn't make the best of impressions.

Topics to avoid

First of all, avoid questions which the interviewer may expect you to already have the answers to. This includes questions about the organisation which a quick look at their website could have answered. You'll expose a lack of preparation.

It's also best to avoid questions about pay and holidays, unless, of course, the interviewer brings up these topics. Such matters can always be covered in later discussions. Bringing them up during your interview can place too much focus on what you are expecting from the employer rather than what you are offering them. This is never a good idea at this stage in the process.

You should also avoid asking questions which the interviewer is unlikely to know the answers to. They won't take kindly to this at all! Your interviewer may well work within a centralised HR department whose staff can't be expected to know the precise operational details of every other department.

TOP TIP

Whatever questions you select, be aware that they can reveal a lot about you; the way you think, your motivations, needs etc. Remember this and try to keep your questions upbeat and positive.

What NOT to ask

It's hard to give precise advice as to what questions not to ask because it will depend on the specific circumstances. However, here's a selection of examples which it will generally not be appropriate to ask:

➤ How long have you been in business/operating for?

➤ Who founded/owns the company?

➤ Who are your main competitors?

➤ How is this industry/sector evolving?

➤ What is the salary on offer?

➤ When could I expect a pay review?

➤ How many days paid holiday do I get?

➤ Will I be expected to work overtime?

➤ If I work overtime, will I get time off in lieu?

➤ Is there sick pay?

➤ Do you provide childcare?

➤ What other perks are there in the package on offer?

➤ Are there any non-compete clauses in the contract?

➤ Have you made any redundancies recently?

➤ How did I do?!

➤ Which bus should I get to go to . . .?

Wrapping up

In wrapping up, make sure that you find out when you can expect to hear whether or not you have been successful, it could be anything from the same day (in which case, you may even be asked to wait around for a decision) to a couple of weeks. Don't ever be tempted to ask the interviewer if they felt the interview went well; it smacks of desperation. I heard of one candidate who even admitted to the interviewer that they didn't feel the interview had gone very well and they asked if perhaps there were any other jobs going elsewhere in the organisation. Don't let nerves get the better of you.

And finally, remember to thank the interviewer for their time before you leave.

Chapter **8**

The 15 most common interview mistakes – and how to avoid them!

The same common mistakes crop up time and time again at interview. Too many jobseekers miss out on their dream job because of a small number of easily avoided blunders.

Some of the mistakes that people make at interview are very obvious and others are more subtle. The CV Centre® has conducted a comprehensive survey to derive a 'Top 15' and, in this chapter, I will list these 15 most common interview mistakes. As always, forewarned is forearmed.

1. Not knowing enough about the job you're applying for

The key to preventing pre-interview jitters is to prepare thoroughly. We fear what we don't know and what we can't control, yet there is much you can do to plan and prepare for your interview, and the first item on your list should be to thoroughly research the job in question.

Not knowing the ins and outs of a job is among the worst blunders you can make in an interview, as is failing to demonstrate to the interviewer how you meet the requirements for the job.

If you are to be able to convince a recruiter that you are right for the role then you need to first get clear in your own mind why you are right for the role, and you can't do this unless you have properly researched and understood what it will involve.

2. Not knowing enough about the organisation you're applying to

A number of popular interview questions are designed to probe and assess your knowledge of the organisation to which you are applying. An interviewer will expect you to have done your homework. If you're unprepared and unable to adequately answer these questions then it's going to be a big black mark on your application.

Just as a lack of knowledge of the job will count against you, a lack of knowledge of the organisation will betray a lack of effort on your part. How can they be sure you really want this job and that you're really the right candidate for the job if you know so little about their organisation?

3. Arriving late

The importance of making appropriate travel arrangements to get to your interview may seem obvious. However, this is frequently a problem for candidates. Being late for an interview – even by only a few minutes – is a very common mistake but it will immediately count against you.

STATISTIC

Nearly half of recruiters won't give a candidate a job if they are more than 10 minutes late for interview, regardless of how well they perform.

It's also important to arrive early, and allow yourself time to relax and compose yourself.

4. Lacking enthusiasm

Whilst there's obviously a fine balance here, enthusiasm in an interview is essential just don't overdo it. Recruiters often find that the person they are interviewing lacks enthusiasm and this will count against you. Sometimes it might just be due to nerves and shyness, but don't let this happen to you. Be enthusiastic – and show it.

Confident people inspire confidence in others; if you appear confident that you are able to do the job, the employer is likely to be more inclined to believe that you can, and lacking in enthusiasm is generally fatal to your chances of success.

5. Arrogance

Whilst confidence is critical to a successful interview, it is important not to go to the other extreme and appear overconfident or arrogant, which is a surprisingly common mistake. You simply need to appreciate what your strengths are and to value yourself accordingly.

6. Dressing inappropriately

Presentation, presentation, presentation

The way you physically present yourself will make an impression on an interviewer before you even have a chance to open your mouth.

Present yourself professionally and the interviewer will see you as a professional; the opposite also applies. Never forget that you are marketing yourself, and the way you present yourself can have an impact on the interviewer almost as powerful as what you have to say.

Presentation can make all the difference between success and failure. Image is everything.

STATISTIC

Research has shown that your interviewer could well have made up his or her mind about you within just 30 seconds of having met you. Use this to your advantage.

7. Poor body language

Recruiters are trained to make informed assessments of candidates, not only based on how they communicate verbally but on how they communicate physically.

Even if your interviewer has received no formal training, they are going to be inherently sensitive to certain nuances of body language just like the rest of us. It's instinctive.

The importance of body language as a factor in the decision-making process should not be underestimated. Recruiters regularly complain about candidates' poor body language – limp handshakes, lack of eye contact, slouching and failing to smile.

8. Poor first impressions

First impressions are extremely important. Interviewers can reach a decision about a candidate very quickly. Make a poor first impression and you might not be able to recover from it. How quickly do you sum up someone you've just met? It's probably less than a couple of minutes.

Remember: you never get a second chance to make a first impression.

Too many candidates turn up reeking of smoke or garlic – or worse.

9. Answering the wrong question

It's surprisingly easy for your thoughts to stray elsewhere and for you to fail to properly listen to a question. You're in a stressful situation and you have a lot on your mind; it's possible to get distracted.

Interviewers often have to deal with candidates going off at a tangent and giving the answer to a totally different question from the one that was asked.

Listen and engage your brain before opening your mouth.

I talk more about the basic principles of handling interview questions in Chapter 1: Essential principles.

10. Failing to sell yourself effectively

Far too many candidates fail to sell themselves effectively at interview; giving boring, monosyllabic answers unsupported by any real-life examples.

It's essential for you to think through and create your own answers to potential questions. Wherever possible, try to integrate real-life examples into your answers rather than just speaking hypothetically. Flagging up specific, relevant examples from your own experience is an ideal way of reinforcing your points in the interviewer's mind.

More about this in Chapter 1: Essential principles.

11. Being a parrot

Many candidates at interview make the mistake of sounding as if they're reciting from some old-fashioned book called *101 Interview Questions.*

Make sure you don't fall into this trap. This is really important. There are no universally right answers to interview questions just answers that are right for *you.*

And even if you have prepared and memorised your own answers, you should be careful to make sure that your delivery is natural and doesn't come across as rehearsed.

This important topic is discussed in greater detail in Chapter 1: Essential principles.

12. Lying

Never lie at interview or say something that you cannot substantiate.

For many candidates their troubles start even before they've been invited for the interview because a large percentage of people seem to think it's permissible to tell a few small porkies when writing their CV. Many think it's acceptable because 'everyone else does it', and many prospective employers do not check an applicant's information as thoroughly as they perhaps should.

However, I would always strongly caution anyone against telling anything but the truth on their CV. You can easily come unstuck during an interview as a result.

STATISTIC

Surveys show that approximately 30 per cent of candidates 'lie' to one degree or another at interview.

For a longer discussion on this topic, please refer back to Chapter 1: Essential principles.

13. Being critical of others

Having problems with the boss is the top reason people give (in surveys) for changing jobs. However, you should never say anything negative about either a current or a previous employer.

Criticising your current employer is considered one of the top mistakes you can make at interview and will most likely cost you the job regardless of whether or not your criticism is justified.

Likewise, you should avoid criticising current or former colleagues.

There are a number of different interview questions you need to look out for on this front:

Question 3 in Chapter 2: The top 10 interview questions.
Questions 14, 26 and 27 in Chapter 3: Fifty more classic questions: be prepared.
Questions 5 and 10 in Chapter 4: The top 25 tough questions: taking the heat.

14. Failing to ask your own questions

As I mentioned in Chapter 7, interviews are a two-way process. So make sure you have your own questions ready for the end of the interview. You're almost certain to be asked: 'Do you have any questions for me/ us?' Take this as another opportunity to demonstrate your interest and enthusiasm. Fail to take it and you risk undoing all the good work you've done. Check out the Statistic box in Chapter 7 to see what happens to such candidates.

15. Prematurely talking money

As I said earlier, avoid asking questions about pay and holidays unless the interviewer brings up these topics. If you raise them, you'll be perceived as focusing on what you're expecting from the employer rather than what you're offering them. Better to leave these subjects for later discussions.

Of course, the interviewer may ask you questions about pay, and if you'd like advice on how to handle this then take a look at Questions 47 and 48 in Chapter 3: Fifty more classic questions: be prepared.

16. Not following up after the interview

Yes, I know I said this chapter would cover the 15 most common interview mistakes, but everyone loves a bonus, don't they?

So here's a 16th mistake for you: not following up after the interview. Big mistake. But help is at hand . . .

Keeping track of your interviews

We've put together a spreadsheet to help you keep track of the interviews you attend – who with, what date etc. Not only that, it'll let you keep track of the CVs you have sent out as well.

This tracking tool will help you to know exactly whether and when to follow up on an application, and it will prevent you from becoming confused. Much better to keep yourself organised and this Excel spreadsheet will enable you to do just that. To download your free copy, please visit: **www.jamesinn.es**

The Interview Book

If you would like to learn more about interview technique in general, above and beyond just how to handle interview questions, then please take a look at my comprehensive book on the subject, *The Interview Book*. You can place your order for a copy via our website: **www.jamesinn.es**

Conclusion

Successfully passing an interview is not rocket science. Most of what I have outlined is reasonably simple to take on board and it's just a matter of putting in the necessary time and effort.

I hope you have found *The Interview Question & Answer Book* useful. Don't forget to visit our website: **www.jamesinn.es**

GOOD LUCK!

What did you think of this book?

We're really keen to hear from you about this book, so that we can make our publishing even better.

Please log on to the following website and leave us your feedback.

It will only take a few minutes and your thoughts are invaluable to us.

www.pearsoned.co.uk/bookfeedback

Further reading and resources

Recommended books

Borg, J. (2013) *Persuasion: The Art of Influencing People*, 4th edition, Harlow: Pearson

Fagan, A. (2013) *Brilliant Job Hunting*, 3rd edition, Harlow: Pearson

Hodgson, S. (2014) *Brilliant Answers to Tough Interview Questions*, 5th edition, Harlow: Pearson

Innes, J. (2015) *The Cover Letter Book*, 3rd edition, Harlow: Pearson

Innes, J. (2015) *The CV Book*, 3rd edition, Harlow: Pearson

Innes, J. (2015) *The Interview Question & Answer Book*, 2nd edition, Harlow: Pearson

Innes, J. (2012) *Ultimate New Job*, London: Kogan Page

Jay, R. (2010) *Brilliant Interview*, 3rd edition, Harlow: Pearson

Yeung, R. (2013) *Confidence*, 3rd edition, Harlow: Pearson

These titles are available in all major bookshops. You can also learn more about them and even place an order for a copy by visiting our website:

www.jamesinn.es

Online resources

I keep my list of online resources – online. That way I can keep it bang up to date at all times. Please access our website for a wide range of useful links to job sites and other online resources:

www.jamesinn.es

Chronological index of questions

Index